Poems for Thinking

ROBERT FISHER

Nash Pollock Publishing

First published in 1997 by
Nash Pollock Publishing
32 Warwick Street
Oxford OX4 1SX

9 8 7 6 5 4

Orders to:
York Publishing Services
64 Hallfield Road
Layerthorpe
York YO31 7ZQ

A catalogue record of this book is available from the British Library.

ISBN 1 898255 15 6

Design, typesetting and production management by
Black Dog Design, Buckingham

Printed in Great Britain by The Bath Press, Bath

Poems for Thinking

This book is to be returned on or before
the last date stamped below.

Falkirk Council

Contents

INTRODUCTION

Poetry begins in delight and ends in wisdom – Robert Frost

A poem is like a present in words – Anne, aged 10

Poems for Thinking is a resource aimed at developing the thinking, learning and language skills of children and young students. It offers a collection of poetry to enjoy and think about. The book includes more than thirty poems, traditional and modern, from a variety of cultures, including English, Caribbean, Indian, Chinese, native American, European, Irish and Scottish traditions.

The poems chosen are written to communicate something of importance, and hence are poems for thinking. Each of the poems is followed by a discussion plan of questions to challenge children's thinking about the poem. There is also a discussion plan that raises questions about one theme or key concept explored in the poem. Follow-up activities and further poems are suggested to encourage students to extend their thinking and their response to poems. The book also contains a glossary of terms used in discussing poetry, and an index of the poets represented in the book, giving brief details of their lives and of their poetry.

The poems and discussion plans can be used in a variety of ways, for example as a stimulus for thinking with:

- individual children
- children working in pairs
- small groups within a class
- the whole class as a community of enquiry
- larger groups of children, such as a school assembly.

Poems for Thinking can be used by individuals or groups to create a thinking and learning community in the classroom through questions, discussion, reflective writing, art, drama and other activities that help develop thinking and the use of poetry across the curriculum.

Children should be introduced to a wide range of literature 'with challenging subject matter that broadens perspectives and extends thinking' (*English in the National Curriculum* p13). This literature should include the elements of this book:

- a range of good quality modern poetry
- some classic poetry
- texts drawn from a variety of cultures and traditions.

In addition children should read and respond to a range of fiction, as well as myths, legends and traditional stories (see *Stories for Thinking* in this series). This book focuses on ways of fostering a love of poetry through a range of poems, and ways to enable children to become thoughtful readers able to pose questions, to discuss and to evaluate critically the texts they read.

What is poetry?

One way to begin would be to ask: What is a poem, and how does it differ from a story? There are many possible answers to this question. When a group of eight and nine year olds were asked, Nadine replied: 'A poem is a kind of short story in which the words sometimes rhyme.' For Jodie, 'A poem is a kind of secret message which you have to work out.' For Tom a poem is 'Good ideas said in the fewest words.' For Stuart a poem is not just a story, but is 'a piece of writing that the poet *thinks*.' A poem for these children is a kind of story, with a tale or secret message to unfold. It is told in a few words and might rhyme. Poems differ from stories, as Stuart suggests, because in a poem you have direct access to the thoughts of a poet. In a poem you meet the mind of the poet, person to person, through the words he or she writes.

The poet James Elroy Flecker expressed eloquently the communicative urge of the poet, and the need for understanding, in these words:

> Since I can never see your face,
> And never shake you by the hand
> I send my soul through time and space
> To greet you. You will understand.

> ('To a Poet a Thousand Years Hence')

Poetry expresses thought, feeling or imagination in language which is rhythmic. While prose walks, poems dance. One often needs to listen to a poem to appreciate its rhythm. A poem well crafted will use language to its limits, so to 'tune in' you need time to listen and to think. All children have the ability to enjoy and respond imaginatively to poetry, given the help and encouragement of an enthusiastic teacher. In so doing they will not only be listening to the words, but also seeking to understand the thoughts and feelings of the writer.

'A poem is what's written by a poet,' explained a child. So what do poets say about poetry? The following are some ways in which poets themselves have defined poetry:

What is poetry?   Some reflections on poetry by poets

Poetry is ...

'memorable speech' *W H Auden*

'the shortest way of saying things. It also looks nicer on a page than prose. It gives room to think and dream' *John Betjemen*

'musical thought' *Thomas Carlyle*

'the best words in the best order' *Samuel Coleridge*

'a fresh look and a fresh listen' *Robert Frost*

'the art of uniting pleasure with truth by calling imagination to the help of reason' *Samuel Johnson*

'a way of preserving experience' *Philip Larkin*

'the synthesis of hyacinths and biscuits' *Carl Sandburg*

'about feelings and incidents that have happened in life' *Michael Rosen*

'another way of finding out what life and the world means' *Elizabeth Jennings*

How to begin: feeding the ear

Poetry begins by feeding the ear. Children like to listen to poems. They delight in word sounds and word play. They will read old favourites over and over again and enjoy learning a favourite poem by heart. Children have a natural ear for rhyme and rhythm, and poetry feeds this innate response to the patterns of spoken language. The love of poetry begins in the delight of shared word play. The gift of words, wrapped in riddles, rhymes and poetry is an enduring gift. Research shows that a rich diet of nursery rhyme is a foundation for success in learning to read. The task for teachers is to help children move on from a love of simple rhyme to an appreciation of poetry that will feed the mind as well as the ear. But many teachers feel daunted by this task. So, how to begin?

The secret of introducing children to poetry is simple. Like learning a language the best way is immersion. Simply plunge in and share with children the poetry you like, and do it often. Teaching poetry turns out to be simpler once one is doing it. 'A poem a day' is a simple recipe, but reading just one poem a day to a class or a child will create a rich resource of language experience. Giving children a varied range of poetry books to look at and discuss, asking them to choose their favourites to have read out, will help begin that process of learning to be discerning readers, writers, listeners and speakers.

Extending the range

I only like funny poems that rhyme and tongue twisters – child, aged 10

One reason why children like poems is that they are usually short. Poems come in small packages of words. Most poems do not take long to read - a boon for children still struggling with reading. The rhythmic patterns and repetitions of poems make it easier to read and learn verse than prose. But children can easily become trapped in 'kid's verse' and funny rhymes. Once children are at ease with poetry, and have a heritage of rhymes that are familiar and 'belong' to them as part of life in school and home, we should extend the range by offering the stimulus of new and challenging poems drawn from past and present, near and far.

Poetry began as a communal experience that grew out of an oral tradition of shared stories, songs and chants. The vocal pattern of a poem, like its meaning, is not fixed, though it is more or less constrained by its written form. A poem can be read aloud in many ways (and is thus a good vehicle for teaching punctuation). Poetry includes many forms, styles and cultural elements. Students should have experience of poetry from a range of cultures and times, including our own.

Today we are richer in poetry than ever before. More good poets are writing poetry for children, and we have more access to the poetry of other times and cultures than before. Poets female as well as male, living as well as dead, from all cultures, including famous and the ordinary people (nearly everyone has written some poetry or song at some time), both adults and children (more and more children's poems are being published) are part of this living tradition. The storehouse of poetry is an embarrassment of riches, but amongst this great outpouring there is much dross alongside the gold. This book aims to help children in this sorting process to create a context and a language for responding to poetry in both critical and creative ways – and so help them create their own heritage of poetry to nourish them through life.

Why read poetry?

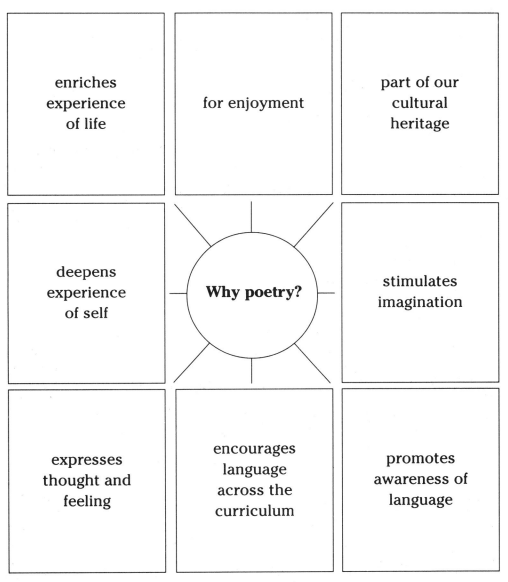

Poetry is one of the best ways we have of expressing thoughts and feelings. Poems are the expressions of an individual experience. They make public what was private. The meaning of a poem is not fixed. When a reader experiences a poem it is in a sense re-created anew, from the given elements of the text and from the personal experience and understanding of the reader. If children are to deepen their understanding of poetry, they need help in creating meaning from the given words and images, and in relating these to their own experience. Hence the two kinds of discussion plan offered after each poem, one exploring meanings in the text and one exploring personal response to a key theme taken from the text.

People are afraid of poetry because they think there is a right answer. 'A poem', as Seamus Heaney says, 'is something that can stand being kicked around by you and me.' The poet wrote it, you read it and make if you can something of it. This is not like the search for a 'right' answer. To understand poetry means, as Keats said, being 'capable of being in uncertainties, mysteries, doubts, without any irritable reaching after fact and reason.' Poems lack the detailed context and lines of reasoning of other kinds of writing. This is what makes them open to a range of interpretations and explanations. Good poems demand as much as they give. They have layers of meaning, and need to be interrogated. They need to be read and re-read, questioned and reflected on if they are to yield their meanings. This process of digging into a poem stimulates the imagination, and offers a model for our own creative expression.

Responding to poems

I like it, but I don't know why – child, aged 8

Reading, responding to and writing poems can enable children to voice thoughts and feelings that might otherwise remain trapped, inarticulate and unspoken. Poetry can empower children by offering them many voices, many messages, many tongues - echoed in the words of Whitman:

> Give me the song of a sound unsung,
> Give me the heart of a child that is young,
> Give me friends I can stretch among,
> Give me the words and give me the tongue.

We need to listen attentively to the sound of the poem, and to tell students not to worry about words they do not understand – but to try to get a sense of the poem as a whole, and to listen to the music of the words. We must not expect a poem to surrender all its secrets at a first reading. Encourage students to read carefully a second or third time, stopping at the end of each sentence to see if they have understood the meaning or feeling being expressed. It may be helpful to read in pairs or in small groups so that each can benefit from the response of others.

We might begin by asking students to pay attention to the title of the poem. Does it give any clues as to what the poem is about? Does it suggest how the poem might be read? Much of the meaning of a poem is how we say it. Can the poem be said in different ways?

There is no one way of thinking about a poem. How do we help students find ways of making sense of poetry? The following are some questions that may help in making sense of a poem. They are not exhaustive of all possible questions, but illustrate ways of focusing attention on some aspects of a poem.

Some questions to ask about any poem:

Questions about the poem (first thoughts)
- Was there anything interesting, strange or puzzling about the poem?
- What do you remember about the poem?
- If you were telling someone about this poem what would you say?

Questions about personal response to the poem
- What does the poem make you think?
- What does the poem make you feel?
- What do you like or dislike about the poem?

Questions about the poet
- Who is speaking or writing the poem?
- What does the poem tell us, if anything, about the poet?
- Why was the poem written?

Questions about the language used in the poem
- What kind of language is the poem written in?
- Is there anything special or strange about the words used in the poem?
- Do the words create any pictures or images in your mind?

Questions about the form of the poem
- What makes this piece of writing a poem?
- What kinds of pattern does the poem make?
- What kind of lines/stanzas/rhymes/rhythms are used?

Questions about the meaning of a poem
- What is the theme of the poem?
- What does the poem tell you?
- What is the poet trying to say?

Questions about the type of poem
- What kind of poem is this? How would you describe this kind of poem?
- Do you know other poems like this (similar in form or theme)?
- How does it compare with other poems you know?

These and other questions model ways in which we want students to ask themselves in their critical response to texts. The most important questions will be those that the students themselves ask about the poem. The best questions are those that leave room for more than one answer and invite different viewpoints.

Thinking time

It takes me time to think – child, aged 10

One of the best ways to generate questions and discussion of a variety of viewpoints is to create a Community of Enquiry (see below) about the poem. The most useful preliminary to this kind of whole class discussion is to have individual thinking time followed by paired or small group discussion (a 'think-pair-share' approach). This enables participants to express tentative responses and explore ways of articulating thoughts in a relatively relaxed way. The first questions above ('first thoughts') may be helpful in the early stages of coming to grips with a poem.

You are likely to have your own views about the central theme of the poem, and a theme for discussion is suggested after each poem in the book. There is a danger in seeing yourself (or this book) as the authority for deciding the true meaning of a poem. The readings of others may reveal the true heart or the unexpected aspects of the poem, which is why inviting a range of responses through a Community of Enquiry can be rich and rewarding.

One of the problems in responding to poetry at any age is knowing what you want to say. Making notes or jottings can help. Many writers keep a notebook or journal to jot down initial responses. These tentative thoughts, which may not make sense to others, may be the basis for more articulate ideas later. If they are not recorded they may get lost, either forgotten or overtaken by the thoughts of others. These thoughts can be written in a personal notebook or 'Thinking Book', or annotated on a copy of the poem.

Children need time and space to 'digest' a poem. After the reading give them a Thinking Time in which to write down words, phrases, thoughts and feelings as they occur, without editing or worrying about spelling. Responses to a poem in a student's journal need not be in words; they may be better captured in a sketch, or in a combination of words and drawings. What shapes might we draw to describe the poem?

On a copy of the poem students might be invited to highlight key words or phrases. Notes on the sheet should be kept simple, and different colours could be used in lines, loops and arrows to help analyse different elements of the poem. The following are some of the things to look for in annotating a poem:

> ### *Annotating a poem*
>
> On a copy of the poem use coloured pens to make notes, for example:
> * to underline the most effective word in each line
> * to circle the most interesting or puzzling image or idea
> * to link any rhymes
> * to note other sound patterns: alliteration, assonance and rhythm
> * to show repetitions of words, images, ideas
> * to identify connections between different parts of a poem
> * to sketch ideas in a realistic or abstract way
> * to ask questions about the poem

An advantage of annotating poems in this way is that an acetate sheet for an overhead projector showing the complete poem can be used by the teacher to collect and share the patterns, repetitions and observations about the poem found by the group.

This initial Thinking Time in a space of silence provides the groundwork for subsequent writing or discussion. The poet D H Lawrence saw poetry as a means of using thought to explore one's personal experience. He wrote:

> Thought, I love thought,
> But not the jiggling and twisting of already existent ideas,
> I despise that self-important game.
> Thought is the welling up of an unknown life into consciousness,
> Thought is the testing of statements on the touchstone of conscience,
> Thought is gazing on to the face of life, and reading what can be read.
> Thought is pondering over experience, and coming to a conclusion.
> Thought is not a trick, or an exercise, or a set of dodges,
> Thought is a man in his wholeness wholly attending.

One way to follow up a session of 'sweet silent thought' is to share ideas through brainstorming. Invite students to call out their ideas, questions and comments in relation to the given poem. The result should be a collection of thoughts, ideas and words recorded on a large sheet of paper as a basis for further class discussion, creating in the classroom what has been called a Community of Enquiry.

The following are some of the questions raised for discussion by a class of eight year olds using the poem 'Parrot' by Alan Brownjohn (p 91) as a stimulus:

1 Why do they expect the parrot to talk? (Kiran)
2 How do they know the parrot can talk? (Kevin)
3 How do they know the parrot thinks? (Michael)
4 What does he mean by 'olive green and sulky'? (James)
5 Why do they think that he thinks those things? (Katherine)
6 Why do they think he thinks? (Katia)
7 How do they know he is listening? (Kayley)
8 Why do they think he is a 'thinking bird'? (Georgina)
9 Why do they think he ponders all he hears? (Kiran)

From their list of questions written up on a board the children chose what they thought was the most interesting for a forty minute kind of classroom discussion called a Community of Enquiry.

Discussing poems in a Community of Enquiry

A Community of Enquiry is a method of organising classroom discussion within a particular moral and rational framework. Children and their teacher share reading or listening to a poem. Students are given thinking time to devise their own questions and discuss them. They express ideas and to listen to what others say. With practice their discussions become more disciplined and more focused. Through listening and discussing with others they develop deeper understanding of language and of literature, and of themselves as thinkers and readers.

In a Community of Enquiry there are certain moral principles and ground rules of behaviour that make discussion possible and which should be honoured at all times. Among the behaviours that are expected to become the norms of the group are:

1 *Attentive listening* – paying close attention to one another's words and showing care, respect and consideration by observing the rules of discussion such as 'only one speaks at a time' (OOSAT).
2 *No put-downs* – appreciating others, making helpful contributions and avoiding negative remarks, name-calling, hurtful gestures or behaviour.
3 *Right to pass* – choosing when to participate in group discussion and activity, having the right to silence within the a group setting.

4   *Being reasonable* – giving reasons, evidence and examples in support of views and being willing to allow what others say to influence their views.

5   *Being truthful* – speaking what they believe to be true, not deliberately lying, deceiving or pretending to believe what they do not believe.

6   *Having the courage of one's convictions* – feeling free and confident enough to express a personal opinion.

7   *Ensuring equal opportunities* – creating equal opportunities to speak and to have the attention of others, not allowing the dominance of the few.

8   *Respecting others* – respecting the rights and opinions of others, giving attention and thought to what they say, responding with care for them as persons.

9   *Being patient* – allowing others time to think, speak and respond.

10 *Being open-minded* – being open to the opinions of others, willing to suspend judgement and to change one's view.

The rules for discussion should be agreed by the groups and expressed in their words, and could be posted in a prominent place in the classroom. They underline the importance of teacher and peer role modelling in teaching interpersonal skills and caring behaviour. In focusing on children's social development they aim to create the moral and social context for discussion.

The common format for this is to sit in a circle, with the teacher as part of the circle, leading the group in a sharing activity. Experience in this large group provides an opportunity to model the norms we hope the child will follow in other, smaller learning groups. The virtue of a circle is that everyone can see the face of every other member – and can talk person to person with any other member.

The benefits that a teacher can bring to an enquiry or learning conversation include the following elements of mediation:

*   *focusing* eg by directing attention to important points, issues or factors in discussion

*   *seeking meaning* eg by asking for reasons, explanation or clarification of ideas

*   *expanding* eg by showing links between ideas, and links to new ideas for discussion

*   *discouraging* the tendency of students to focus on their own ideas rather than responding to and building on the ideas of others

- *rewarding* eg by verbal or non-verbal expressions of positive response every positive contribution to the discussion.

One of the purposes of the teacher as participant is to get pupils to talk and listen to each other, rather than directing all their talk through the teacher. This aim of helping children feel independent and equal in their responses to each other is central to creating a Community of Enquiry. Children may however feel intimidated or vulnerable, or feel they lack the appropriate discourse, in discussing poetry with an adult present. The chance first to discuss the poem with a partner or small group can help to alleviate this anxiety. The strategy of 'think-pair-share', is recommended as it moves from individual to paired and then whole group discussion.

Certain characteristics or logical conditions define discussion, and these can help us, and children, to review and evaluate the success of discussion. Questions to assess whether genuine discussion has taken place include:

1   *Talking* – have we talked to one another?

2   *Listening* – have we listened to each other?

3   *Responding* – have we responded to what others have said?

4   *Considering viewpoints* – have we considered more than one pont of view?

5   *Thinking and learning* – have we developed our ideas, knowledge or understanding?

These conditions define what discussion is, but they are matters of degree. All discussion involves different kinds of interaction, and in the classroom the quality of these interactions can be seen to develop and improve over time, for example by students talking more, listening more attentively, responding more to what others say, putting forward more divergent points of view, and being able to correct and refine their judgements to develop their thinking.

Poems for Thinking - what is a typical lesson?

The following is a suggested sequence of activities for using a poem for thinking as a stimulus for a community of enquiry for one or more lessons:

1 The poem is read aloud. The poem may be read again by teacher or student.

2 Students read the poem to themselves and are given 'thinking time' to reflect on the poem.

3 After reading the poem, ask the students what they found interesting or curious in the poem, and to choose an idea they would like to discuss.

4 Invite students to ask questions. Their questions or comments are written on the board, with the name of the contributor written alongside their question.

5 Choose a question from the board, perhaps by voting, to form the basis of a discussion.

6 Begin the discussion by inviting the person whose question is chosen to say why they asked that question, and invite others to respond.

7 Extend children's thinking through asking further questions during or after the discussion (sample questions are given after each poem).

Follow-up activities

Invite students to extend themes from the poem through other activities such as writing, drawing or drama (suggested activities are given after each poem).

Allow opportunities for students to review and share what they have learnt at the end of each session or unit of work.

Encourage students to find their own poems for thinking and sharing for a future lesson.

Extending the experience of a poem

Can a picture of a poem be a poem? – child, aged 11

One way to extend the experience of a poem is to provide further activity that invites students to make their own creative response to the theme or the poem. After each poem a number of further activities are suggested, as well as further poems to research and respond to.

The following are activities that can be used to extend the student's experience of poetry through branching out from a poem. Students can:

• collect poems for an anthology or display related to a theme or poet

- illustrate the poem by drawing, painting or making a three-dimensional model
- tape record the group discussion of a poem, to share and review later
- plan, prepare and present an individual or group reading of a chosen poem
- search through a selection of poetry books to find their own chosen Poem for Thinking
- close their eyes during a reading to visualise the poem in their 'mind's eye'
- explore the poem through movement and mime eg by creating a still picture or tableau
- design an informative poster to advertise the poem or poet
- create a collage of words, quotations and/or pictures about a theme or poet
- make a mask or masks linked to the theme or poem
- brainstorm and mind-map words associated with a theme, image or idea in a poem
- write a letter to the poet, with any questions you have about the poem
- visit a library to review, survey and choose poetry books
- invite a guest to discuss and share their favourite poems and to share yours
- learn a chosen poem by heart: discuss the best ways of learning poems
- compare and discuss two poems by the same poet or on the same theme
- list the similarites and differences between two poems
- create and discuss your own title for a given untitled poem
- predict the words missing in a copy of a poem which has some words deleted (cloze)
- reconstruct the line or verse order of a poem which has had lines or verses jumbled
- put into poetic form a poem that has been written as prose
- use a poem for dictation practice, students to add their own punctuation
- create music or sound effects to accompany a spoken poem
- write poem in a calligraphic style to best express the poem's theme
- listen to two or more taped readings of a poem: discuss which you prefer and why

- decide if some 'wrong' words have been put in a poem, and propose alternatives
- display their own pictures of poems: can others match pictures to poems?
- tell the poem as a news story: what happened before/during/after the poem?
- devise questions about the poem to test the listening skills of others
- write a review of the poem, quoting favourite or least favourite parts
- annotate dictionary definitions of the hardest words to help younger readers
- hunt parts of speech in a poem, underlining eg nouns, verbs etc in different colours
- choose their five favourite poems, share and discuss choices (including least favourite)
- invite a poet to share, discuss and be questioned about their poetry
- investigate poetry clues - locate poems in books from given fragments of verse

The experience of poetry can also be extended through poetic writing. The advantage of writing over talking is that what you write can become permanent, can be shaped and altered and can be shared with a wide range of audiences. The poems in this book can become models and a stimulus for the writing of poetry.

> 'And as imagination bodes forth
> The form of things unknown, the poet's pen
> Turns them into shapes, and gives to airy nothing
> A local habitation and a name.'

(William Shakspeare, from *A Midsummer Night's Dream*)

How do we help children to take up 'the poet's pen', to think and write their own poems?

Writing poems

Dylan Thomas, the Welsh poet, when he was a schoolboy was one day caught playing truant from school. 'Where are you going, boy?' asked the teacher who spotted him. 'I'm going to write poetry ', said Dylan. 'Well.' said the teacher, 'make sure you don't get caught!'

Children become writers of poetry through thinking about the poetry they read. As they read and discuss poetry the words and ideas they encounter will inform their writing. They will often remember the rhythm of words, the shape and forms of the poetry they have experienced. Their favourite poems will be the poems they know. They will begin to make use of what they absorb when writing their own poems. That is one reason why the poetry they experience should be rich, varied and of good quality.

Any poem can become a model for the student's own writing, either by borrowing the pattern or using the subject matter as a stimulus for their own ideas. Confidence can quickly be gained by following simple poetic forms like haiku. More able children will often depart from a given framework and initiate new patterns. The following is an acrostic poem written on the death of a pet:

Gentle rodent in its cage
Under the apple tree
It was a pet given to me
Named Poochie
Every day it squeaked
Ate anything it could get
Paper, grapes, grass and hay
It died early one morning
Garden its grave.

Jake, aged 8

Christina Rossetti's poem 'What is Pink?' (p 73) could be the stimulus for writing colour poems. Asking children to write not about things that are the colour but about what the colour makes them think and feel. The following is a poem written after a discussion about colour:

Red

Red is an anchor that burns in my soul,
but you never noticed the pain.
You knew I loved you when we were together.
Oh I wonder why I can't seem to make things right.
I see you in my dreams,
I can't let it go.
Don't you see I care for you.
Oh I wonder why love is a red anchor that hurts me.

Laura, aged 8

It is not enough to give children a theme or a framework to work from in writing a poem. They also need some guidelines, for example:

1 *Poems don't have to rhyme.*

Rhymes can give a poem rhythm but few children manage strictly rhymed verse succesfully. They give too much attention to finding a rhymed word rather than to find the best word for flow and meaning. It is better for them to say what they really want to say rather than get stuck in trying to find a rhyme.

2 *Think where lines begin and end.*

To make their writing look like a poem on the page ask them, or help them, to start a new line whenever they pause for breath. Talk about how line breaks help the reader know how the poet wants the poem read.

3 *Say something new.*

A poem should have something new in it. Encourage children to find words only they would use, and to say something that will surprise the reader.

4 *Write the fewest words in the best order.*

Every word in a poem should be there for a purpose, any word you don't need should be cut out. Get rid of unnecessary 'ands', 'thens', sos' and 'thes'. Think about the order of words. Can you say the same thing in a different way. Which way sounds best?

All poets draft and redraft their work to try to make it better - better words, better order of words, and better ideas. The poet Paul Valery said 'a poem is never finished, only abandoned.' W B Yeats revised his published poems for each new edition. Children need to know that redrafting is not something they do because they are at school, but because it is something all writers do. It is not that everything must be re-written, but that parts may be improved.

A typical writing lesson will include a starting point to stimulate discussion, followed by writing, reviewing and possible redrafting of parts of the work. The final version can then be shared, and published for a wider audience. The following list summarises each stage in this process:

A writing session

Starting point   A stimulus chosen by teacher, child or group eg using a poem as a model, shared experiences, curriculum work, close observation of objects, visual images, feelings, imagination, senses, people, places etc.

Discussion	*Child* - gathers words, ideas, and decides on the form to use. *Teacher* – encourages, questions, creates the atmosphere, making the task manageable.
Writing	*Child* – composes words, ideas, form; either alone or with partner or group. May redraft to improve parts, or ask partner to make helpful suggestions. *Teacher* – supports eg helps brainstorm words and ideas, prompts, questions, helps with planning and problems of spelling, handwriting, punctuation, grammar, layout. May write alongside child.
Reviewing	*Child* – reads the finished writing. May share it with partner. *Teacher* – responds to content; identifies successful words, ideas, images; reviews any weak parts or surface errors; and praises positive features. May ask child to edit or redraft where needed.
Sharing	*Child* – reads and/or displays poem. May publish poem for wider audience in the school, at home or in the community. *Teacher* – provides time and materials for poem to be well presented, and opportunity for writing to be read, heard and responded to by others.

Poetry is about the carefully crafted use of language. The teacher's job is to help the child exercise this control. If the finished poem reads more like prose, look at the words to see if any can be left out. Ask the child to read the poem to a friend or response partner. Encourage the partner to give an honest but helpful response, for example can they find two good things to say about the poem, and one thing to improve? Is there a line that doesn't quite work, or a dull word that could be replaced with an interesting one? Does the poem sound good when it is read out? Becoming more experienced critics of each other's work will help them with their own writing.

The most important response to the poem will be that of the teacher or other significant adult. Any response should therefore begin and end with encouragement (a 'praise sandwich', with any critical suggestions being the filling in the middle). Elements to consider in assessing a poem, whether it be a child's, your own or a published poet's, include the following:

• Is the poem interesting?
• Is it imaginative?

- Does it make you think?
- How well has the writer structured the poem?
- How good is the choice of words?
- Does it use rhyme or rhythm?
- Does it use any poetic techniques?

(See the glossary p 107 for a range of poetic techniques and terms.)

The best model a child can have is a teacher who reads poetry and writes poetry, and can share this experience with the child. This may mean writing in front of the children, on a board or large piece of paper, perhaps making up a class poem together, or reading aloud an example of your own writing, or drafting your own poem while the children are writing theirs. This demonstrates not only how writing might be tackled, but also makes a good opportunity for discussing what makes effective writing. In the end the best poem for thinking might be your own.

Poems

1

To Find a Poem

To find a poem
listen to the wind
whispering words strange and rare
look under stones
5   there you might find a fossil
shape of an old poem.
They turn up anywhere
in the most unexpected places
look for words that are trapped
10   in the branches of trees
in the wings of birds
in rockpools by the sea.
And if you find one
handle it carefully
15   like an injured bird
for a poem can die
or slip through the fingers
like a live eel
and be lost in the stream.
20   Follow whatever footprints are there
even if no-one else can see them
for clues to lost poems
are waiting to be found
round the next corner
25   or before you right now.
You may have just missed one
never mind
look again tomorrow
you may find your poem
30   or your poem
lost somewhere in the dark
may be waiting for you.

Robert Fisher

Thinking about the poem

Key question: What does the poem mean?

1 What is the poem about?
2 Is 'To Find a Poem' a poem? Why do you think it is, or is not, a poem?
3 Are there any rhymes in this poem? If there are, can you say where there are rhymes?
4 What does it say you should do to find a poem?
5 What does it mean by saying poems can be found (line 1)?
6 Where does it say poems can 'turn up' (line 7)?
7 What does it mean that poems should be handled carefully (line 14)?
8 In what way can a poem 'die' or 'be lost' (line 19)?
9 In what ways can a poem be 'waiting to be found' (line 23)?
10 What does it mean by saying a poem may be waiting for you (lines 29-33)?

Thinking about a poem

Key question: What is a poem?

1 Why do people write poems?
2 What is a poem? Could a poem be one sentence, or one word? Why, or why not?
3 Could a poem be as long as a book? Could it be endless – or beginningless?
4 Do poems have to rhyme? Could a poem rhyme at the beginning or middle of a line?
5 Must a poem be written in words? Could it be made in paint, music or in other ways?
6 Could silence be a poem? Could a poem be a noise? If so, can you give an example?
7 Could living things like trees, birds, an animal or a person be a poem?
8 Could something in nature be a poem, like the sea, a waterfall or rainbow?
9 Is the meaning of a poem what the poet who writes it thinks it is, or what the person who reads it thinks it is?
10 Can everyone write or enjoy poems, or only special people? Can you give a reason?

Further activities

- Make an anthology of your favourite poems to give, or share with others.
- Learn a chosen poem; see if you can remember it to say to others.
- Create a poster poem by writing and illustrating a chosen poem on a large piece of paper.
- Hold a poetry party where people can read their favourite poems to each other.
- Write what you think about poems. You could begin: 'A poem is ...'

Further poems for thinking

Other poems by Robert Fisher to read and think about include: 'Uncle Fred' in *Ghosts Galore*, ed. Robert Fisher (Faber); 'Minotaur' in *Amazing Monsters*, ed. Robert Fisher (Faber); and 'Metamorphosis' in *Minibeasts*, ed. Robert Fisher (Faber).

Other poems about poetry include: 'Dis Poetry' by Benjamin Zephaniah, 'Poetry' by Kit Wright and 'After the Book is Closed' by Gerard Benson.

2

A Sea Shell

See what a lovely shell,
Small and pure as a pearl,
Lying close to my foot,
Frail, but a work divine,
5   Made so fairly well
With delicate spire and whorl,
How exquisitely minute –
A miracle of design!

What is it? A learned man
10   could give it a clumsy name
Let him name it who can –
the beauty would be just the same.

Alfred, Lord Tennyson

A thing of beauty is a joy forever;
Its loveliness increases; it will never
Pass into nothingness; but still will keep
A bower quiet for us, and a sleep
Full of sweet dreams, and health, and quiet breathing.

John Keats (from *Endymion*)

Thinking about the poem

Key question: What does the poem mean?

1   The poem begins; 'See what a lovely shell...' Who do you think the poet is talking to?
2   What makes the poet think that the sea shell is lovely?
3   What does it mean to say the shell is as 'pure as a pearl' (line 2)?
4   Where do you think the poet is when he sees the shell?
5   What does 'a work divine' mean?
6   The shell is said to be made so 'fairly' well (line 5). Is 'fairly' a proper word? What does it mean?
7   What is a 'delicate spire and whorl'? Can you explain it or draw it?
8   Why is the shell called 'a miracle of design' (line 8)? Is it designed? Why, or why not?

9   What is a shell? Do you know the names of any shells? Where does the name come from? What is a 'clumsy' name (line 10)?

10   Do you agree that shells are beautiful? Why?

Thinking about beautiful things

Key question: What does beauty mean?

1   What things are beautiful? Are people beautiful? In what ways?

2   When something is beautiful, is every part of it beautiful?

3   Does everyone agree what is beautiful and what is not beautiful? Why?

4   Is beauty only concerned with what things look like?

5   Do you think a blind person can appreciate beauty?

6   Can something very small be beautiful? Give an example.

7   Can something very big be beautiful? Give an example.

8   Is there some way in which all beautiful things are alike?

9   There is an old saying: 'Beauty is in the eye of the beholder'. What does this mean? Is it true?

10   What is the most beautiful thing you have ever seen? Why was it beautiful? How did it make you feel?

Further activities

• Make a collection of sea shells. Let each take a turn to choose and say which shell they think is most beautiful.

• Design your own shell (or make a close observational drawing of a real shell). Give it a special name.

• Write a poem or description about the most beautiful thing you have ever seen.

• Draw pictures of a beautiful and an ugly fish or bird. Show and discuss the pictures. Are they beautiful and ugly? What makes them beautiful or ugly?

• Read and discuss the story of the Two Painters (in *Stories for Thinking* p 27).

Further poems for thinking

Other poems by Tennyson to read and think about include: 'The Kraken', 'The Lady of Shalott', and 'Flower in the Crannied Wall'.

3

Back in the Playground Blues

Dreamed I was in a school playground, I was about four feet high
Yes dreamed I was back in the playground, and standing about four
    feet high
The playground was about three miles long and the playground
    was five miles wide

It was broken black tarmac with a high fence all around
5   Broken black dusty tarmac with a high fence running all around
And it had a special name to it, they called it the Killing Ground.

Got a mother and a father, they're a thousand miles away
The Rulers of the Killing Ground are coming out to play
Everyone thinking who they going to play with today?

10   You get it for being Jewish
Get it for being black
Get it for being chicken
Get it for fighting back
You get it for being big and fat
15   Get it for being small
O those who get it get it and get it
For any damn thing at all

Sometimes they take a beetle, tear off its six legs one by one
Beetle on its black back rocking in the lunchtime sun
20   but a beetle can't beg for mercy, a beetle's not half the fun

Heard a deep voice talking, it had that iceberg sound;
'It prepares them for life' – but I have never found
Any place in my life that's worse than the Killing Ground.

Adrian Mitchell

Thinking about the poem

Key question: What does the poem mean?

1   The poem is called: 'Back in the Playground Blues'. What does 'blues' mean?

2   The poem begins 'Dreamed ...' In what sense do you think it is about a dream?

3   What was the playground like?

4   Why does the poet call the playground The Killing Ground?

5   Who do you think the Rulers of the Killing Ground might be?

6   Who do you think is in the playground?

7   What does the poet mean by 'You get it ...' in lines 11-15?

8   Why is a beetle 'not half the fun'? How is a beetle different from a human?

9   Who do you think says 'It prepares them for life' (line 22)? Do you agree?

10 Why do you think the poet 'never found any place in life worse than the Killing Ground'?

Thinking about bullying

Key question: What does bullying mean?

1   What is a bully?

2   Why do some people want to bully or pick on other people and make them unhappy?

3   Are there different kinds of bullying? If so, what kinds are there?

4   Do you know anyone who has been bullied? Give an example.

5   Have you ever been bullied? What happened?

6   Have you ever bullied someone else? If so why, if not why not?

7   What advice would you give to someone who was being bullied?

8   What would you say to a bully to try to persuade them to stop bullying?

9   What could people in a school do to stop bullying happening?

10 There is a saying 'Sticks and stones can break my bones but words can never hurt me'. Do you think this is true? Why?

Further activities

- Write a poem or story about what happens in the playground.
- Make a large frieze showing all the activities that happen in the playground.
- Create a play about an incident of bullying.
- Interview people about their worst fears.
- Listen to some 'blues' or rap songs. Write your own blues or rap song. You could begin: 'I got up this morning and was feeling rather bad ...'

Further poems for thinking

Other poems by Adrian Mitchell to read and think about include: 'Pause', 'Dumb Insolence', and 'Not a Very Cheerful Song I'm Afraid'.

Other poems about bullying include: 'The Bully Asleep' by John Walsh, 'The Bully' by Fay Maschler and, '1945' by Geoffrey Summerfield.

4

The Road Not Taken

Two roads diverged in a yellow wood,
And sorry I could not travel both
And be one traveller, long I stood
And looked down one as far as I could
5   To where it bent in the undergrowth;

Then took the other, as just as fair,
And having perhaps the better claim,
because it was grassy and wanted wear;
Though as for that the passing there
10   Had worn them really about the same,

And both that morning equally lay
In leaves no step had trodden black.
Oh, I kept the first for another day!
Yet knowing how way leads on to way,
15   I doubted if ever I should come back.

I shall be telling this with a sigh
Somewhere ages and ages hence:
Two roads diverged in a wood, and I –
I took the one less travelled by,
20   And that has made all the difference.

Robert Frost

Thinking about the poem

Key question: What does the poem mean?

1   Where do you think the poet might have been going?

2   The poem says: 'Two roads diverged' (line 1). What does 'diverged' mean? What do you know that diverges?

3   What do you think the wood in the poem was like? How would you describe the wood?

4   Why did the 'other' road look better? Was it really better, do you think? Why?

5   What time of year do you think it was? Are there any clues to this in the poem?

6   What did the poet intend to do on another day (line 13)? Do you think he did? Why?

7   Why did the poet think he would never come back?

8   Who do you think he will tell about the two roads that diverged in the wood (line 16)?

9   Why will he be telling this 'with a sigh' (line 16)?

10   When he says taking the road less travelled by 'made all the difference' (line 20), what do you think he means?

Thinking about choice

Key question: What does making a choice mean?

1   What choices do you have in your life? What are the most important choices you make?

2   What is the hardest choice you have ever made? Why was it so hard?

3   What was the easiest choice you ever made? Why was it so easy?

4   What was the worst choice you ever made? Why was it so bad?

5   What was the best choice you ever made? Why was it so good?

6   Is it best to choose for yourself, or to consult others about what to choose? Why?

7   Are there some things you would like to choose in your life but are not free to choose?

8   Do you find it easy to make up your mind when making a choice? Give an example.

9   What advice would you give to someone who could not make up their mind?

10   Who tries to influence what you choose? How do they try to influence you? Give an example.

Further activities

- Find out about decision trees. Make a decision tree eg about choosing a pet.
- Investigate the ways advertisers try to influence your choice.
- Select two things of the same kind eg objects, pictures, poems. Show them to pairs or groups to choose their favourite. Identify the criteria they are using.
- Discuss or act out a moral dilemma. Give reasons for what you should or would choose to do.
- Brainstorm and list the criteria you would use to choose a common product such as book, article of clothing or party menu.

Further poems for thinking

Other poems by Robert Frost to read and think about include: 'Stopping by Woods on a Snowy Evening', 'The Runaway', and 'Mending Wall'.

5

How Can You Buy the Sky?

How can you buy the sky?
How can you own the rain and wind?

My mother told me,
Every part of this earth is sacred to our people.
5   Every pine needle. Every sandy shore.
Every mist in the dark woods.
Every meadow and humming insect.
All are holy in the memory of our people.

My father told me,
10   I know the sap that courses through the trees
as I know the blood that flows in my veins.
We are part of the earth and it is part of us.
The perfumed flowers are our sisters.
The bear, the deer, the great eagle, these are our brothers.
15   The rocky crests, the meadows, the ponies – all belong to the same
    family.

The voice of my ancestors said to me,
The shining water that moves in the streams and rivers
is not simply water, but the blood of your grandfather's
    grandfather.
Each ghostly reflection in the clear waters of the lake
20   tells of memories in the life of our people.
The water's murmur is the voice of your great-great-grandmother.
The rivers are our brothers. They quench our thirst.
They carry our canoes and feed our children.
You must give the rivers kindness
25   you would give to any brother.

The voice of my grandfather said to me,
The air is precious. It shares its spirit with all the life it supports.
The wind that gave me my first breath also received my last sigh.
You must keep the land and air apart and sacred,
30   as a place where one can go to taste the wind
that is sweetened by the meadow flowers.

When the last Red Man and Woman have vanished with their
    wilderness,
and their memory is only the shadow of a cloud moving across the
    prairie, will the shores and forest still be here?
Will there be any of the spirit of my people left?
35   My ancestors said to me, This we know:
The earth does not belong to us. We belong to the earth.

Chief Seattle

(Chief Seattle spoke these words in 1855 when the US government wanted to buy
the lands of his native American people. His words have been transcribed and
interpreted many times since.)

Thinking about the poem

Key question: What does the poem mean?

1   To whom is Chief Seattle speaking when he asks the questions in lines
    1 and 2?

2   What does he mean by asking how you can buy the sky, or own the
    rain or wind?

3   What did his mother tell him? Why has he remembered her words?

4   What did his father tell him? Why has he remembered his words?

5   What do you think 'the voice of my ancestors' means (line 16)? Is it a
    real voice? Whose voice?

6   What did the voice of his ancestors tell him? Did he invent or
    remember these words?

7   What did the voice of his grandfather say? Why does he think the air
    is precious?

8   What is the 'spirit' of the air? What does it mean to say it is 'sacred'
    (line 29)?

9   What does the last line mean?

10   The words were spoken by Chief Seattle, and written down by
    someone who could translate what he said into written English. Do
    you think it is a poem? Why?

Thinking about conservation

Key question: What does conserving nature mean?

1   Do you think that parts of our world, the planet Earth, are alive? Can you give examples?

2   If parts of our world are alive, does it mean that the whole world is alive?

3   Do you think the earth has a spirit? Explain why or why not.

4   Are humans and animals part of the planet Earth, or are they simply living on it?

5   In what sense is water the life blood of the planet?

6   What are the dangers that face the quality of our air and water? What causes pollution?

7   Why do we have to use nature?

8   Why shouldn't we use nature just as we please?

9   How could we help to conserve and improve our local surroundings or neighbourhood?

10   Should we help to conserve the resources of our living world? Why? How?

Further activities

• Display and discuss pictures, posters and research work on the sources of pollution.

• Investigate ways and devise plans for improving some aspect of the local environment.

• Design anti-litter posters or litter bins, survey local litter and devise anti-litter measures.

• Study the world's endangered species and habitats.

• Write for information from, or interview, a representative of a conservation organisation.

Further poems for thinking

An extended version of Chief Seattle's message can be found in *Brother Eagle, Sister Sky*, a beautifully illustrated picture book by Susan Jeffers (Puffin). Other poems on the theme of conservation to read and think about can be found in *What on Earth: Poems with a Conservation Theme* (Faber) and *Earthways, Earthwise: Poems on Conservation* (Oxford University Press) both edited by Judith Nicholls.

6

The Tyger

Tyger! Tyger! burning bright
In the forests of the night,
What immortal hand or eye
Could frame thy fearful symmetry?

5   In what distant deeps or skies
Burnt the fire of thine eyes?
On what wings dare he aspire?
What the hand dare seize the fire?

And what shoulder, & what art,
10   Could twist the sinews of thy heart?
And when thy heart began to beat,
What dread hand? & what dread feet?

What the hammer? What the chain?
In what furnace was thy brain?
15   What the anvil? what dread grasp
Dare its deadly terrors clasp?

When the stars threw down their spears,
And water'd heaven with their tears,
Did he smile his work to see?
20   Did he who made the Lamb make thee?

Tyger! Tyger! burning bright
In the forests of the night,
What immortal hand or eye,
Dare frame thy fearful symmetry?

William Blake

Thinking about the poem

Key question: What does the poem mean?

1   Do you prefer to read the poem or have it read to you? Why?
2   Do you have to understand all the words to like a poem? Are there words in this poem you do not understand?
3   What do you find curious, strange or puzzling about the poem?
4   What is it about a tiger that is 'burning bright' (line 1)?
5   What does 'fearful symmetry' mean (line 4)?
6   What questions does the poet ask in this poem?
7   Who is the poet speaking to?
8   Is this writing a poem? Why?
9   What shows this poem was written long ago?
10   Why do you think Blake wrote this poem?

Thinking about creation

What does creation mean?

1   What does it mean to create something? Is creating more than just making?
2   Have you created anything? Give an example.
3   Are you able to create something new every day? What makes it new?
4   Can you create happiness and laughter? How?
5   Can you create sadness and sorrow ? How?
6   Can you create something through music, art or drama?
7   Can you create ideas through thinking? Give an example.
8   What is the difference between creation and invention?
9   Was the world was created? If so, can you say how?
10   Can you help to create a better world? If so, how?

Further activities

* Read myths and legends about the creation of the world.
* Create a frieze showing the creation of the world, such as the Biblical version of creation.
* Display an example of something that each person in the group has created.
* Listen to some music from Haydn's *Creation*.
* Study Blake's illustrated print of his 'Tyger' poem. Make your own illustrated version.

Further poems for thinking

Other poems Blake by to read and think about include: 'The Fly', 'Jerusalem', 'The Poison Tree', 'The Smile', and 'Auguries of Innocence'.

7

The Twa Corbies

As I was walking all alane
I heard twa corbies making a mane;
The tane unto the t'other say,
'Where sall we gang dine today?'

5   'In behint yon auld fail dyke,
I wot there lies a new-slain Knight;
And naebody kens that he lies there,
But his hawk, his hound, and lady fair.

'His hound is to the hunting gane,
10   His hawk to fetch the wild-fowl hame,
His lady's ta'en another mate,
So we may mak' our dinner sweet.

'Ye'ell sit on his white hause-bane,
And I'll pick out his bonny blue een:
15   Wi' a lock o' his gowden hair
We'll theek our nest when it grows bare.

'Mony a one for him makes mane,
But none sall ken where he is gane;
O'er his white banes, when they are bare,
20   The wind sall blaw for evermair.'

Anon Scottish ballad

Note: corbies = crows
      fail-dyke = turf wall
      hause-bane = neck bone
      theek = thatch

Thinking about the poem

Key question: What does the poem mean?

1   Who do you think is speaking this poem?
2   Where does this poem take place?
3   What words tell you it is written in a Scots dialect?
4   Which words do you not know the meaning of? What do you guess their meaning might be?
5   Who knows where the 'new-slain knight' lies?
6   What might explain why or how they know?
7   Where has his hawk and hound gone? Where has his lady gone?
8   What do the corbies intend to do? Why?
9   Who do you think will mourn the death of the knight?
10   What kind of poem is this? What is your favourite line?

Thinking about death

Key question: What is death?

1   How do we feel when someone dies?
2   It can be very sad when someone dies. How do people show their sadness?
3   How can you help someone who is feeling very sad?
4   What helps us to remember people who have died?
5   What is mourning? Why do people mourn? Why is it important?
6   Do animals have a different attitude to death from humans? Why is this?
7   What is an obituary? What would you want people to say about you if you died?
8   Some people believe there is life after death. Do you? Can you explain why?
9   Is it possible to live forever? Would it be a good thing?
10   Some people say it is wrong to talk about death. What do you think?

(*Note:* Death is viewed in various ways in different cultures and religious traditions, and may be associated with grief for children who have suffered bereavement. There may be many unexpressed thoughts and feelings about death, and children may have their own grief to share. Discussion about death should not be avoided but should be handled with sensitivity.)

Further activities

- Research burial customs in different cultures eg in ancient Egypt.
- Draw (or design) a memorial to somebody famous.
- Visit a local churchyard or cemetery. Record what you see, feel and think.
- Write an obituary, elegy or epitaph for a chosen hero, human or animal, who has died.
- Read and discuss 'The boy who wanted to live forever' (in *Stories for Thinking* p 40).

Further poems for thinking

Other ballads for thinking include: 'Lord Randal', 'Mad Tom's Song' (version by Robert Graves), 'The Strange Visitor', and 'A Lyke-Wake Dirge' (see also p 99).

Other poems about death for thinking include the ballad 'The Unquiet Grave', 'Song' by Christina Rossetti, 'Requiem' by R L Stevenson, 'Epitaph' by Walter de la Mare, and 'The Tree and the Pool' by Brian Patten.

8

The Hairy Toe

Once there was a woman went out to pick beans,
and she found a Hairy Toe.
She took the Hairy Toe home with her,
and that night, when she went to bed,
5   the wind began to moan and groan.
Away off in the distance
she seemed to hear a voice crying,
'Where's my Hair-r-ry To-o-oe?
Who's got my Hair -r-ry To-o-oe?'

10   The woman scrooched down,
way down under her covers,
and about that time
the wind appeared to hit the house,

smoosh,

15   and the old house creaked and cracked
like something was trying to get in.
The voice had come nearer,
almost at the door now,
and it said,
20   'Where's my Hair-r-ry To-o-oe?
Who's got my Hair-r-ry To-o-oe?'

The woman scrooched further down
under the covers
and pulled them tight around her head.
25   The wind growled around her house
like some big animal
and r-r-rumbled
over the chimbley.
All at once she heard the door cr-r-a-ack
30   and Something slipped in
and began to creep over the floor.

The floor went
cre-e-eack, cre-e-eack
at every step that thing took towards her bed.

35 The woman could almost feel
it bending over her bed.
There in an awful voice it said:
'Where's my Hair-r-ry To-o-oe?
Who's got my Hair-r-ry To-o-oe?
40 YOU'VE GOT IT!"

Anon (Traditional American)

Thinking about the poem

Key question: What does the poem mean?
1 Where did the woman find the Hairy Toe?
2 Why do you think she took it home with her? Was this wise?
3 Do you think she really heard a voice crying, 'Where's my Hairy Toe?'
4 Was she scared by the voice? What makes you think so?
5 What do you think the Something in line 30 might have been?
6 Why did the woman think it was a 'Something'?
7 What do you think the voice sounded like?
8 What do you think happened after the poem ends?
9 Do you think this poem is better read or spoken? Why?
10 What makes this a poem? What is special about this poem? Who do you think 'Anon' was?

Thinking about fear

Key question: What is fear?
1 What scares you? Why does it scare you?
2 How does it feel being afraid? How would you describe it?
3 Are there some things it is good to be afraid of? Why? Can you give examples?
4 Are there some things it is silly being afraid of? Can you give examples?
5 Can you stop yourself feeling scared? How do you stop yourself feeling scared?
6 Is being scared a good reason for not doing something? Why? Can you give an example?
7 Can you think of something you used to be afraid of but are not any more? Why is this?
8 Why do different things frighten different people?
9 Can things that aren't real be scary? Why is this?

10 Is there a difference between fear and being scared? Can you be
brave and feel afraid or scared?

Further activities

- Draw or paint the scariest thing you can think of. Explain your picture
  to others.
- Ask volunteers to describe their scariest experience, what happened,
  how they felt and what they did.
- Choose a scary experience and act or mime it in groups of four or five.
- Tell a scary chain story, with each person adding a few sentences to
  develop the story.
- Play a scary piece of music and describe what the music made you
  think and feel.

Further poems for thinking

Other poems about being scared to read and think about include: 'The
Longest Journey in the World' by Michael Rosen, 'Who's That?' by James
Kirkup, 'I Once Dressed Up' by Robert Fisher, and other poems in *Ghosts
Galore* ed. R. Fisher (Faber).

9

Friends

I fear it's very wrong of me,
And yet I must admit,
When someone offers friendship
I want the whole of it.
5   I don't want everybody else
To share my friends with me.
At least, I want one special one,
Who, indisputably,

Loves me much more than all the rest,
10   Who's always on my side,
Who never cares what others say,
Who lets me come and hide
Within his shadow, in his house –
It doesn't matter where –
15   Who lets me simply be myself,
Who's always, always there.

Elizabeth Jennings

Thinking about the poem

Key question: What does the poem mean?

1   What is the poet admitting in this poem (line 2)?
2   How do people offer friendship (line 3)?
3   Why do you think the poet does not want anyone else to share her friends (lines 5/6)?
4   What does 'indisputably' mean (line 8)? What things are indisputable?
5   What does the poet want her special friend to be like?
6   What does to 'hide within his shadow' (line 13) mean?
7   How can someone be 'always, always there' (line 16)?
8   What makes this a poem?
9   Is there anything special about the way the two verses of the poem are written?
10 Do you like this poem? Why, or why not?

Thinking about friends

Key question: What does being friends mean?

1   Do you prefer to have one special friend, or to have many friends?

2   Does a friend have to like you more than he or she likes other people?

3   Can you talk a lot and play with someone and not be a friend?

4   Can people who do not talk or play together be friends?

5   Can you argue, quarrel or fight with someone and still be a friend? Why, or why not?

6   Is it possible never to argue or quarrel with someone? Would that person be a friend?

7   Can people be happy without friends?

8   Can you be afraid of a friend? If so, give an example; if not why not?

9   Can you be a friend of someone you have never met? If so, give an example; if not why not?

10   What is the difference between friends and family?

Further activities

• Make a mind-map about FRIENDS. Write the word in the middle of a large page and add connect it to all the words you can think of related to FRIEND.

• Find and share your favourite story or poem about friends.

• Describe your best friend in the class. See if people recognise your friend from your description.

• Research the stories of famous friendships, such as the Biblical friendships of David and Jonathan (1 Samuel 18), or Ruth and Naomi (Ruth).

• Read a story, questions and further activites about friendship in *Stories for Thinking* pp 50-52.

Further poems for thinking

Other poems by Elizabeth Jennings to read and think about include: 'The Secret Brother', 'My Animals', and 'A Classroom'.

Other poems about friends include: 'Friends' by Robert Service, 'Sometimes It Happens' by Brian Patten, 'Friends' by Gareth Owen, 'About Friends' by Brian Jones and 'Love and Friendship' by Emily Bronte.

10

The Happiness of Fish

Chuang Tzu and Hue Tzu
were walking on the bridge
over the Hao river.

Chuang said:
5 'See how the small fish
leap and dart about.
That is the happiness of fish.'

Hue replied:
'Since you are not a fish
10 how can you know
the happiness of fish?'

Chuang said:
'Since you are not I
how can you know
15 that I do not know
the happiness of fish?'

Hue replied:
'If I, not being you,
cannot know what you know,
20 it follows that you,
not being a fish,
cannot know the happiness of fish.'

Chuang said:
'Wait! Let us go back
25 to your original question.
You asked me how I know
the happiness of fish.
The words of your question
show you knew that I know
30 the happiness of fish.

I know their happiness
from my own happiness
as I walk over the bridge
and see them leap and play.'

Chuang Tzu , China (translated by Robert Fisher)

Thinking about the poem

Key question: What does the poem mean?

1   Who do you think Chuang Tzu and Hue Tzu were?
2   What did Chuang Tzu see from the bridge?
3   Why did Chuang think the fish were happy?
4   What did Hue think?
5   What did Chuang say to try to persuade Hue that he could not know what Chuang knew?
6   Do you think Chuang's argument was a good one? Why?
7   What did Hue say to try to persuade Chuang he was wrong?
8   Do you think Hue's argument was a good one? Why?
9   At the end of the poem how does Chuang explain how he knows the happiness of fish?
10   Do you think that Chuang was right in saying he knew that the fish were happy? Why?

Thinking about happiness

Key question: What does happiness mean?

1   What does it mean to be happy? Can you give examples of being happy?
2   When you say you are happy, how do you know you are happy?
3   Do you know when other people are happy? Do you know if animals are happy?
4   Is feeling you are happy the same as knowing you are happy?
5   If you are not happy, are you unhappy? Are there differerent kinds of happiness?
6   Do you always know how you are feeling?
7   Can someone else really know how you are feeling?
8   Could you be happy all the time? Why, or why not?
9   Are you always happy when you are playing?
10   Can other people make you happy or can you only make yourself happy? Explain.

Further activities

- Create a Happiness chart by brainstorming a concept map of synonyms for happiness.
- Draw your own visual representation or metaphor for happiness.
- Write a poem on the theme of happiness. It could begin: 'Happiness is ...'.
- Discuss, write or record your happiest memory.
- Write a recipe for a happy life, a happy home or happy school.

Further poems for thinking

Other poems about hapiness to read and think about include: 'A Birthday' by Christina Rossetti, 'In Just-spring' by ee cummings and 'Sally' by Phoebe Hesketh. See also *Pangur Ban*, p 51.

11

Who Do You Think You Are?

Who do you think you are
    and what do you think you came from?
From toenails to the hair of your head you are
    mixed of the earth, of the air,
5   Of compounds equal to the burning gold and amethyst
    lights of the Mountains of the Blood of Christ at Santa Fé.
Listen to the laboratory man tell what you are
    made of, man, listen while he takes you apart.
Weighing 150 pounds you hold 3.500 cubic feet of gas –
10   oxygen, hydrogen, nitrogen.
From the 22 pounds and 10 ounces of carbon in you
    is the filling of 9000 lead pencils.
In your blood are 50 grains of iron and in the rest
    of your frame enough iron to make a spike
15   that would hold your weight.
From your 50 ounces of phosphorous could be made
    800,000 matches and elsewhere in your physical
    premises are hidden 60 lumps of sugar, 20 tea-
    spoons of salt, 38 quarts of water, two ounces
20   of lime, and scatterings of starch, chloride of
    potash, magnesium, sulphur, hydrochloric acid.
You are a walking drug store and also a cosmos and
    a phantasmagoria treading a lonesome valley,
    one of the many people, one of the minions and
25   myrmidons who would like an answer to the
    question, 'Who and what are you?'
One of the people seeing sun, fog, zero weather,
    seeing fire, flood, famine, having meditations
        On fish, birds, leaves, seeds,
30   Skins and shells emptied of living form,
        The beautiful legs of Kentucky thoroughbreds
        And the patience of army mules.

Carl Sandburg

Thinking about the poem

Key question: What does the poem mean?

1   How would you answer the first question in the poem, 'Who do you think you are'?

2   How would you answer the second question in the poem, 'and where do you think you come from'?

3   Who is the poet speaking to? Why is he asking these questions?

4   What is a compound (line 5)? What compounds does the poet say you are made from?

5   Who is the 'laboratory man' (line 7)? Why does he give these answers?

6   What are all the different elements the poem says you are made from?

7   Why are you a 'walking drug store'?

8   In what ways are you like 'a cosmos', a 'phantasmagoria' or a 'lonesome valley'?

9   What makes this a poem? Is there anything special about the way it is written?

10   What does 'having meditations' mean in the last verse? Do you have any meditations?

Thinking about human beings

Key question: What does it mean to be human?

1   What is a human being? How do you know you are a human being?

2   Do you have to ask someone else to find out what you are? Why? Who?

3   Is knowing what you are the same as knowing who you are?

4   Do you need other people to tell you who you are?

5   Is it possible to become someone else?

6   Are you in some ways different from every other person?

7   Do you ever try to be like someone else? Why?

8   Why might you want to be different? In what ways?

9   What would it be like if everyone was the same?

10   Which are most important – the differences or similarities between people? Why?

Further activities

- Look in a mirror. Make a close observational drawing of what you see.
- Try to change the way you look. Dress up as someone else.
- Make up a new name and character for yourself. Write your autobiography as this person. Make a passport for this person.
- Tape record a conversation between people you know. Listen to the recording and try to identify each person from from their voices.
- Write a poem with the title 'Who do you think you are'? or a story about someone who woke up to find they were somebody else.

Further poems for thinking

Other poems by Carl Sandburg to read and think about include: 'Yarns', 'Wilderness', 'Elephants are Different to Different People', 'Gargoyle', 'Wars' and 'The People, Yes'.

12

Pangur Ban

I and Pangur Ban, my cat,
'Tis like a task we are at;
Hunting mice is his delight,
Hunting words I sit all night.

5   Better far than praise of men
'Tis to sit with book and pen;
Pangur bears me no ill will,
He too plies his simple skill.

'Tis a merry thing to see
10   At our tasks how glad are we,
When at home we sit and find
Entertainment to our mind.

Oftentimes a mouse will stray
In the hero Pangur's way;
15   Oftentimes my keen thought set
Takes a meaning in its net.

'Gainst the wall he sets his eye
Full and fierce and sharp and sly;
'Gainst the wall of my knowledge I
20   All my little wisdom try.

When a mouse darts from its den,
O how glad is Pangur then!
O what gladness do I prove
When I solve the doubts I love!

25   So in peace our tasks we ply,
Pangur Ban, my cat and I;
In our arts we find our bliss,
I have mine and he has his.

Practice every day has made
30   Pangur perfect in his trade;
I get wisdom day and night
Turning darkness into light.

Anon

(Written in Gaelic by an Irish student of the monastery of Carinthia on a copy of St Paul's Epistles, in the eighth century, translated into English by Robin Flowers)

Thinking about the poem

Key question: What does the poem mean?

1 Who is Pangur Ban?
2 In what ways does the poet think Pangur Ban is like him?
3 What is Pangur Ban's 'simple skill' (line 8)? What makes it a skill? What is a skill?
4 Why does the poet like to sit 'with book and pen' (line 6)? What do you think he is doing?
5 What is the 'entertainment' (line 12) to the mind of Pangur Ban, and of the poet?
6 In what ways is what Pangur Ban and the poet are doing similar and different?
7 What could the words ''Gainst the wall of my knowledge I all my wisdom try' (lines 19-20) mean?
8 What are the 'arts' of Pangur Ban and the poet (line 27)? What is an 'art'?
9 What might the last line: 'Turning darkness into light' mean?
10 What is special about this poem? What is puzzling about it?

Thinking about humans and animals

Key question: What should the relationship between humans and animals be?

1 Who owns a pet? What sorts of animals can be pets?
2 What makes a cat like Pangur Ban a pet?
3 Are there some things all pets have in common?
4 Can any animal be a pet?
5 Why do people have pet animals? Do you think people want or need to have pets? What is the difference between wanting and needing?
6 Do people love their pets? Can animals love people?
7 Do we have duties towards our pets? What duties? Why? Do our pets have any duties towards us?
8 Should we look after all animals, including wild animals?
9 Do we know what animals think or feel? Can we tell what they think or feel?
10 In what ways are humans and animals alike? In what ways are they different?

Further activities

- Research and record the kinds of pets that your friends have.
- Interview an animal expert such as pet shop owner, zookeeper or animal charity worker about their relationship and experience with animals.
- Make a close observational drawing of a cat or other pet animal.
- Write a story or monologue imagining your life as a pet animal.
- Write a poem about you and your favourite pet animal.

Further poems for thinking

Other poems about humans and animals to read and think about include: 'My Cat Geoffrey' by Christopher Smart, 'Better Be Kind to Them Now' by D J Enright and 'Pet Shop' by Louis Macneice. These and other poems about pets appear in *Pet Poems* ed. R. Fisher (Faber).

13

A Poem Just for Me

Where am I now I need me
Suddenly where have I gone?
I'm so alone here without me
Tell me please what have I done?

5   Once I did most things together
I went for walks hand in hand
I shared my life so completely
I met my every demand.

Tell me I'll come back tomorrow
10   I'll keep my arms open wide
Tell me that I'll never leave me
My place is here by my side.

Maybe I've simply mislaid me
Like an umbrella or key
15   So that until the day I come my way
Here is a poem just for me.

Roger McGough

Thinking about the poem

Key question: What does the poem mean?

1   When might you need yourself (line 1)?

2   What might it mean to say 'I am so alone here without me' (line 3)?

3   When he says 'Tell me please what have I done?' (line 4) who is the poet talking to?

4   When the poet says 'I shared my life so completely' (line 7), what do you think he means?

5   When he says 'I met my every demand' (line 8), what demands could he mean?

6   I'll never leave me', he says (line 11). Can you leave yourself? How, or why?

7   Can you be mislaid 'like an umbrella or key' (line 14)?

8   What makes 'A Poem Just for Me' a poem? What words are repeated? What rhymes can you find?

9   Is the poet is talking to himself? Do you ever do that? When? Why?

10   What do you like or dislike about this poem?

Thinking about me

Key question: What does 'me' mean?

1   If you know your name, do you know who you are?

2   If you know what you look like, do you know who you are?

3   What makes you different from other people? In what ways are you unique?

4   What makes you the same as other people?

5   How do you know who you are?

6   Could you think you were someone else?

7   Could you think you were more than one person?

8   Is it your body who makes you who you are, or your mind?

9   Could you be a body without a mind, or a mind without a body?

10   Could somebody else be you?

Further activities

• Paint or draw a self portrait.

• Record your physical self eg measure height, length of fingers, head size, pulse rate etc.

• Write an autobiography eg about your family, friends, school, clothes, dreams, hobbies, funniest/most frightening moment, like/dislikes, treasures, hopes for the future etc.

• Research how similar/different you are to other people eg colour of eyes, hair, birthday tastes, kinds of holiday, height, weight etc.

• Write what you would say to yourself if you met yourself for the first time. Write this as a story, poem or conversation.

Further poems for thinking

Other poems by Roger McGough to read and think about include: 'First Day at School', 'The Identification' and 'Bully Night'.

14

It Was Long Ago

I'll tell you, shall I, something I remember?
Something that still means a great deal to me.
It was long ago.

A dusty road in summer I remember,
5   A mountain, and an old house, and a tree
That stood, you know,

Behind the house. An old woman I remember
In a red shawl with a grey cat on her knee
Humming under a tree.

10   She seemed the oldest thing I can remember
But then perhaps I was not more than three.
It was long ago.

I dragged on the dusty road, and I remember
How the old woman looked over the fence at me
15   And seemed to know

How it felt to be three, and called out, I remember,
'Do you like bilberries and cream for tea?'
I went under the tree

And while she hummed, and the cat purred, I remember
20   How she filled a saucer with berries and cream for me
So long ago,

Such berries and such cream I remember
I had never had seen before, and never see
Today, you know.

25   And that is almost all I can remember,
The house, the mountain, the grey cat on her knee,
Her red shawl, and the tree,

And the taste of the berries and the feel of the sun I remember,
And the smell of everything that used to be
30   So long ago,

Till the heat on the road outside again I remember,
And how the long dusty road seemed to have for me
No end, you know.

That is the farthest thing I can remember.
35 It won't mean much to you. It does to me.
Then I grew up, you see.

Eleanor Farjeon

Thinking about the poem

Key question: What does the poem mean?

1 Is there anything special about the first line of the poem? Who is the poet talking to?
2 What does the poet remember about the old woman?
3 Does the poet know how old she was at the time?
4 What does 'long ago' mean? How long ago do you think 'long ago' is?
5 What did the old lady say? Why did she say this?
6 What sounds does the poet remember?
7 What tastes does the poet remember?
8 What smells does the poet mean when she says she remembers 'the smell of everything'?
9 Why do these memories mean so much to the poet? Why has she remembered them?
10 What does the last line mean – 'Then I grew up, you see'?

Thinking about memory

Key question: What are memories?

1 What are your earliest memories? Can you remember how old you were?
2 Do you remember when you started to walk, or to talk?
3 Do you remember the first words you spoke?
4 Do you remember your first friend? Do you remember losing your first baby tooth?
5 Do you remember your first pet animal, your first book, your first toys?
6 Do you remember your first day at school? Are your memories visual, or other senses?

7   Do you remember some things and not others? What makes you remember or not remember?

8   Are there some things you will never forget? Can you choose to remember or forget?

9   Can you remember something that never happened to you? Are all memories true?

10   What do you think happens in your mind when you remember something? How does memory work?

Further activities

- Write or draw your earliest memory.
- Find out what people find easiest to remember – sights, sounds, smells, tastes, or feelings?
- Tell someone everything you can remember about this morning.
- Interview an old person about their earliest memories of childhood and school.
- Play some memory games (see *Games for Thinking* in this series).

Further poems for thinking

Other poems for thinking by Eleanor Farjeon include: 'Mrs. Malone', 'Waking Up' and 'Halloween'.

Other poems about memory include 'I remember, I remember' by Thomas Hood, 'Adlestrop' by Edward Thomas and 'Grandad' by Kit Wright.

See also the story 'Ewongelema' in *Stories for Thinking* in this series.

15

A Boy's Head

In it there is a space ship
and a project
for doing away with piano lessons.

And there is
5 Noah's ark,
which shall be first.

And there is
an entirely new bird,
an entirely new hare,
10 and an entirely new bumble bee.

There is a river
that flows upwards.

There is a multiplication table.

There is anti-matter.

15 And it just cannot be trimmed.

I believe
that only what cannot be trimmed
is a head.

There is much promise
20 in the circumstance
that so many people have heads.

Miroslav Holub

Thinking about the poem

Key question: What does the poem mean?

1 Why is the poem called 'A Boy's Head'? Is it about a real boy?
2 Why do you think there is a 'project for doing away with piano lessons' (line 2/3)? What might that project be?
3 Why do you think there is Noah's ark (line 5)? And in what sense shall it 'be first'?
4 Could there be 'an entirely new bird, hare or bumble bee' (lines 8-10)?
5 What do you think an 'entirely new bird' might be like?
6 Can a river flow upwards (lines 11/12)? Can you think impossible things?

7   What does the poet say 'cannot be trimmed' (lines 15 and 17)?

8   What does the poet say that there is 'much promise' that so many people have heads (lines 19-21)?

9   The poem is called 'A Boy's Head'. What would be another good title for the poem?

10   If a poem was written called 'A Girl's Head' do you think it would be a very different kind of poem? If so, in what ways? If not, why not?

Thinking about mind and brain

Key question: What goes on inside someone's head?

1   What goes on inside your head? What different kinds of thoughts do you have?

2   Do thoughts happen inside your brain? What is a brain?

3   Do thoughts happen inside your mind? What is a mind?

4   Is your mind the same as your brain? Can you say why it is or is not the same?

5   How do you know you have a brain or a mind?

6   Does every living thing have a brain and a mind?

7   Could you have thoughts without a brain? Could you have feelings without a brain?

8   Can you ever know what is going on in someone else's mind? Give an example.

9   Do you think in words, in pictures, or in both? Give examples.

10   When do you have your best thoughts? Where do your best thoughts come from?

Further activities

• Draw what goes on inside your brain. Explain your drawing to others.

• Create a mind map in pairs or small groups. Write 'MIND' in the middle of a page and add all the words you can think of to do with minds.

• Write a story in which the characters are saying one thing but thinking something else.

• Draw a cartoon which shows someone thinking eg draw their thoughts in a speech bubble.

• Write a poem about all the daydreams and strange thoughts that go on in your head.

Further poems for thinking

Other poems by Miroslav Holub to read and think about include: 'Fairy Tale', 'Bullfight', 'A History Lesson' and 'The Door'.

16

Miracles

Why, who makes much of a miracle?
As to me I know of nothing else but miracles,
Whether I walk the streets of Manhattan,
Or dart my sight over the roofs of houses toward the sky,
5   Or wade with naked feet along the beach just in the edge of the
    water,
Or stand under trees in the woods,
Or talk by day with anyone I love, or sleep in the night with anyone
    I love,
Or sit at table at dinner with the rest,
Or look at strangers opposite me riding in the car,
10 Or watch honey-bees busy around the hive of a summer fore-noon,
Or animals feeding in the fields,
Or birds, or the wonderfulness of insects in the air,
Or the wonderfulness of the sundown, or of stars shining so quiet
    and bright,
Or the exquisite delicate thin curve of the new moon in spring;
15 These, and the rest, one and all, are to me miracles,
The whole referring, yet each distinct in its place.

To me every hour of the light and dark is a miracle,
Every cubic inch of space is a miracle,
Every square yard of the surface of the earth is spread with the
    same,
20 Every foot of the interior swarms with the same.

To me the sea is a continual miracle,
The fishes that swim – the rocks – the motion of the waves – the
    ships with men in them,
What stranger miracles are there?

Walt Whitman

Thinking about the poem

Key question: What does the poem mean?

1   What does the first line mean? Who is the poet talking to?

2   The poet says that many things are miracles. Can you find examples of what he thinks are miracles in the poem? How many kinds can you find?

3   The poem says: 'These, and the rest, one and all, are to me miracles' (line 15). What does the poet mean by 'and the rest' ? What might he be thinking of?

4   In the last line the poet asks, 'What stranger miracles are there?' What would you reply?

5   Does this poem rhyme? Do you think poems should rhyme? Why, or why not?

6   This kind of poem is called 'free verse'. What do you think 'free verse' might mean?

7   What words are repeated in the poem? Why are they repeated, do you think?

8   What does the last line of the poem mean?

9   What country do you think Walt Whitman came from? Are there any clues in the poem?

10   This poem is called 'Miracles'. Can you think of another title for this poem?

Thinking about miracles

Key question: What are miracles?

1   What is a miracle?

2   Can you give an example of a miracle? Why is it a miracle?

3   Is a miracle just something that is extraordinary? What are your reasons for thinking that?

4   Is a miracle something that is very unusual? Why, or why not?

5   Has a miracle ever happened in your life? If it has, explain what it was.

6   Can miracles be explained? Give an example of a miracle that can or cannot be explained.

7   Can people believe something is a miracle and be mistaken? Why, or why not?

8   Some people say that only God can perform miracles. Do you agree? Why?

9   If you could perform one miracle what would you choose to do?

10   Do people want miracles in their lives? Why?

Further activities

- Write your own poem about the miracles of everyday life.
- Read about the miracles performed by Jesus, or by other religious leaders.
- Research and perform a medieval Miracle Play.
- Write a story about someone describing something they think is a miracle.
- Invite someone who has been to Lourdes or to another holy shrine where miracles have been reported to talk or be questioned about their trip.

Further poems for thinking

Other poems by Walt Whitman to read and think about include: 'I Think I Could Turn and Live With Animals', 'O Captain! My Captain!' and 'When I Heard the Learn'd Astronomer'.

17

The Listeners

'Is there anybody there?' said the Traveller,
  Knocking on the moonlit door;
And his horse in the silence champed the grasses
  Of the forest's ferny floor:
5 And a bird flew up out of the turret,
  Above the Traveller's head:
And he smote upon the door again a second time;
  'Is there anybody there?' he said.
But no-one descended to the Traveller;
10 No head from the leaf-fringed sill
Leaned over and looked into his grey eyes,
  Where he stood perplexed and still.
But only a host of phantom listeners
  That dwelt in the lone house then
15 Stood listening in the quiet of the moonlight
  To that voice from the world of men;
Stood thronging the faint moonbeams on the dark stair,
  That goes down to the empty hall,
Hearkening an air stirred and shaken
20 By the lonely Traveller's call.
And he felt in his heart their strangeness,
  Their stillness answering his cry,
While his horse moved, cropping the dark turf,
  'Neath the starred and leafy sky;
25 For he suddenly smote on the door, even
  Louder, and lifted his head:–
'Tell them I came and no-one answered,
  That I kept my word,' he said.
Never the least stir made the listeners,
30 Though every word he spake
Fell echoing through the shadowiness of the still house
  From the one man left awake:
Ay, they heard his foot upon the stirrup,
  And the sound of iron on stone,
35 And how the silence surged softly backward,
  When the plunging hoofs were gone.

Walter de la Mare

Thinking about the poem

Key question: What does the poem mean?

1 Who was the Traveller? What does the poem tell us about him? Who might he be?

2 Whose door might he have been knocking on?

3 Why was the Traveller perplexed? What does it mean to be perplexed?

4 The poem says there were 'a host of phantom listeners' (line 13). What is a 'phantom'?

5 Who might the phantom listeners have been?

6 What did the traveller 'feel in his heart' (line 21)? What does it mean to feel something in your heart?

7 The Traveller said to tell them he had come and that he had kept his word (line 28). What do you think he might have meant by saying he had kept his word?

8 Who was the 'one man left awake' (line 32)? In what sense was he the only one awake?

9 Can you tell the story of the poem? Can you solve the mystery of this poem? What happened and why?

10 What makes this a poem?

Thinking about mysteries

Key question: What is a mystery?

1 What is a mystery?

2 What mysteries in life are still to be solved? Give an example. Explain why it is a mystery.

3 If we cannot explain something does it mean it can never be explained?

4 Do you think one day we will be able to explain everything? Why? Would it be a good thing?

5 Have there been any unexplained mysteries in your life? Give an example.

6 Some people put mysterious happenings down to ghosts. Do you think there are such things as ghosts? Explain why.

7 Have you ever read a mystery story? What is a mystery story? Can you give an example?

8 Have you ever heard a mysterious sound? What mysterious sounds you have you heard?

9 What is the best way to solve a mystery?

10 Some people say that God is a mystery. Do you agree?

Further activities

- Listen to Mystery Sounds ie tape recordings of strange sound effects. Describe and discuss what you hear.
- Show and discuss a Mystery Object ie any strange and curious artefact that can be brought in. Draw the object from different angles. Write a description of it.
- Play Mystery Voices. Volunteers hide their eyes and identify someone in the room who speaks to them in a disguised voice (see *Games for Thinking*, p 45).
- Write a mystery story or poem.
- Read a mystery story eg The Marie Celeste (in *Stories for Thinking* p 78) or poem eg 'MacAvity the Mystery Cat' by T S Eliot (in *Old Possum's Book of Cats*).

Further poems for thinking

Other poems by Walter de la Mare by to read and think about include: 'Tom's Angel', 'The Song of the Mad Prince', 'Silver,' and 'Autumn'.

18

Isn't My Name Magical?

Nobody can see my name on me.
My name is inside
and all over me, unseen
like other people also keep it.
5   Isn't my name magical?

My name is mine only.
It tells me I am individual,
the one special person it shakes
when I'm wanted.

10   Even if someone else answers
for me, my message hangs in the air
haunting others, till it stops
with me, the right name.
Isn't your name and my name magic?

15   If I'm with hundreds of people
and my name gets called,
my sound switches me on to answer
like it was my human electricity.

My name echoes across the playground,
20   it comes, it demands my attention.
I have to find out who calls,
who wants me for what.
My name gets blurted out in class,
it is terror, at a bad time,
25   because somebody is cross.

My name gets called in a whisper
I am happy, because
my name may have touched me
with a loving voice.
30   Isn't your name and my name magic?

James Berry
Jamaica/England

Thinking about the poem

Key question: What does the poem mean?

   1   What name does the poem refer to?
   2   When the poet says 'Isn't my name magical?', who is he speaking to?
   3   What does 'My name is inside and all over me' (line 2/3) mean? Is your name 'inside' you?
   4   Is it true when the poet says, 'My name is mine only' (line 6)?
   5   How does a name 'shake' a person when they are wanted (lines 8/9)?
   6   What message 'hangs in the air haunting others' (lines 11/12)?
   7   What is 'human electricity' (line 18)? What causes it?
   8   What might cause a name to be 'terror, at a bad time' (line 24)?
   9   What may be special about a name 'called in a whisper' (line 26)?
  10   Do you think your name is magic? Why, or why not ?

Thinking about names

Key question: Why are names important?

   1   Why do people have names?
   2   What would happen if people didn't have names?
   3   What would happen you didn't have a name? Would you know who you were?
   4   Do some people call you by more than one name? Who? What names? Why?
   5   Do you feel someone different if you're called by a different name?
   6   Has anyone the same name as you? Is your name unique? In what sense is it yours?
   7   Could everyone have the same name?
   8   Could a number be a name? Why, or why not?
   9   Are the names of things different from the names of people? Why, or why not?
  10   Is calling someone by their correct name important? Why?

Further activities

- Ask your parents why they chose your name. Find out why others were given their names.
- Find out how your name is written and spoken in other languages.
- Investigate the origins and meanings of different names eg from a dictionary of names.
- Research naming ceremonies in different religious traditions.
- Read and discuss 'The cat who kept her name' (*Stories for Thinking*, p 81).

Further poems for thinking

Other poems for thinking by James Berry include: 'Benediction' 'Fantasy of an African Boy', 'One', and 'Caribbean Proverb Poems'.

Other poems about names include 'The Naming of Cats' by T.S. Eliot.

See also *My Name My Poem* (ed. J. and C. Curry, Arrow).

19

The Peace Pipe

Gitche Manito, the mighty,
The creator of the nations,
Looked upon them with compassion,
With paternal love and pity;
5   Looked upon their wrath and wrangling
But as quarrels among children,
But as feuds and fights of children!

Over them he stretched his right hand,
To subdue their stubborn natures,
10   To allay their thirst and fever,
By the shadow of his right hand;
Spake to them with voice majestic,
As the sound of far-off waters
Falling into deep abysses,
15   Warning, chiding, spake in this wise:

'O my children! my poor children!
Listen to the words of wisdom,
Listen to the words of warning,
From the lips of the Great Spirit,
20   From the Master of Life who made you!
I have given you lands to hunt in,
I have given you lands to fish in,
I have given you bear and bison,
I have given you roe and reindeer,
25   I have given you brant and beaver,
Filled the marshes full of wild-fowl,
Filled the rivers full of fishes;
Why then are you not contented?
Why then will you hunt each other?

30   I am weary of your quarrels,
      Weary of your wars and bloodshed,
      Weary of your prayers for vengeance,
      Of your wranglings and dissensions;
      All your strength is in your union,
35   All your danger is in discord;
      Therefore be at peace henceforward,
      And as brothers live together.'

Henry Wadsworth Longfellow (from 'Hiawatha')

Thinking about the poem

Key question: What does the poem mean?

1   Who or what is Gitche Manito?
2   Who was Gitche Manito looking at? What was the 'wrath and wrangling' that he looked upon (line 5)?
3   What was his voice like?
4   What was his message to the people he spoke to?
5   What were the questions he asked them?
6   What was he weary of? Why was he weary?
7   What does he mean by saying 'all your strength is in your union' (line 34)? Why does he think that 'All your danger is in discord' (line 35)?
8   What is a peace pipe? What has a peace pipe got to do with the poem?
9   What makes this writing a poem? What is special about its rhythm?
10 What do you like or not like about this poem?

Thinking about quarrels

Key question: What does quarrelling mean?

1   What is a quarrel?
2   Can you remember being in a quarrel? What was it about? Was anyone to blame for the quarrel? Could the quarrel have been prevented? How?
3   Have you ever helped to sort out or end a quarrel? What happened?
4   What is the best way to end a quarrel?
5   Can you be a friend to someone you have quarrelled with? Give an example.
6   What is a feud? Is it wrong for people to quarrel or to feud with each other?

7 What is the difference between a quarrel, a feud and a fight?

8 Why do people quarrel with each other?

9 Why do countries quarrel with each other? Can you give an example of countries quarrelling?

10 What are the advantages of living in peace with other people?

Further activities

• Prepare a shared reading of parts of 'Hiawatha', with movement, music and mime accompaniment.

• Write or act out a quarrel between two or more people.

• Collect and contrast pictures of people at peace and at war (or quarrelling) with each other.

• Study the work of the United Nations, and discuss a current international dispute.

• Choose and listen to your favourite example of peaceful music eg Beethoven's Moonlight Sonata (1st movement).

Further poems for thinking

Other poems by Longfellow to read and think about include: 'The Song of Hiawatha', 'The Children's Hour', and 'My Lost Youth'.

Other poems about quarrels include: 'The Poison Tree' by William Blake, 'Emma Hackett's Newsbook' by Alan Ahlberg and 'The Fight' by Gareth Owen.

20

What is Pink?

What is pink? A rose is pink
By the fountain's brink.
What is red? A poppy's red
In its barley bed.
5 What is blue? The sky is blue
Where the clouds float through.
What is white? A swan is white
Sailing in the light.
What is yellow? Pears are yellow,
10 Rich and ripe and mellow.
What is green? The grass is green,
With small flowers between.
What is violet? Clouds are violet
In the summer twilight.
15 What is orange? Why, an orange,
Just an orange.

Christina Rossetti

What are Heavy?

What are heavy? Sea, sand and sorrow.
What are brief? Today and tomorrow.
What are frail? Spring blossoms and youth.
What are deep? The ocean and truth.

Christina Rossetti

Thinking about the poems

Key question: What do the poems mean?

1 Why do you think these poems are full of questions?
2 The first poem says 'A rose is pink'. Does this refer to any rose or a special rose?
3 Do you agree with the poem when it says 'A poppy's red'?
4 Is the sky blue? Is a swan white? Are pears yellow?
5 Clouds are described as violet 'In the summer twilight'. How would you describe 'violet'?
6 When the poem says an orange is orange, does it mean that nothing else is orange?

7   In what sense are sea, sand and sorrow 'heavy' ('What are Heavy', line 1)?

8   Why are today and tomorrow described as 'brief' (line 2)?

9   What does the poet mean by saying spring blossoms and youth are 'frail' (line 3)?

10   The ocean is deep, but how is truth 'deep' (line 4)?

Thinking about questions

Key question: What is a question ?

1   Why do we ask questions?

2   Do you sometimes get an answer, then ask the same question again? Why?

3   Do you sometimes get different answers to the same question? When, and why?

4   Are some questions better than others? Why? What is a good question?

5   Do you ask yourself a lot of questions? What questions do you ask? Who answers?

6   Do you ever ask yourself a question that you don't know the answer to? Is there a point in doing this?

7   Do you ever ask questions when you know you are not going to like the answer?

8   Do you sometimes ask questions when you already know the answer?

9   Do you sometimes think of questions and not ask them? Why is this?

10   Would you rather ask questions or give answers? Which is more important? Why?

Further activities

• Think up questions about your school, a person you know or things you have to do.

• Think up questions about shapes, sounds or colours.

• Choose a favourite book or story and make up some questions about it.

• Make up your own question-and-answer poem.

• Read and discuss 'The boy who always asked questions' (*Stories for Thinking* p 84).

Further poems for thinking

Other poems by Christina Rossetti to read and think about include: 'A Birthday, Song', 'Something this Foggy Day', 'Uphill' and 'Meeting'.

Other poems about questions include: 'Why?' by Phoebe Hesketh, 'Questions at Night' by Louis Untermeyer, 'I am Just Going Out for a Moment' by Michael Rosen and 'Have You Ever Seen?' by Grace Nichols.

21

I Saw

I saw a peacock with a fiery tail
I saw a blazing comet drop down hail
I saw a cloud with ivy circled round
I saw a sturdy oak creep on the ground
5   I saw an ant swallow up a whale
I saw a raging sea brim full of ale
I saw a Venice glass sixteen foot deep
I saw a well full of men's tears that weep
I saw their eyes all in a flame of fire
10   I saw a house as big as the moon and higher
I saw the sun even in the midst of night
I saw the man that saw this wondrous sight.

I saw a fishpond all on fire
I saw a house bow to a squire
15   I saw a parson twelve feet high
I saw a cottage near the sky
I saw a balloon made of lead
I saw a coffin drop down dead
I saw a sparrow run a race
20   I saw two horses making lace
I saw a girl just like a cat
I saw a kitten wear a hat
I saw a man who saw these too,
And he says, though strange, they all are true.

Anon

Thinking about the poem

Key question: What does the poem mean?

1   The poem is called 'I Saw'. Why do you think it is called 'I Saw'?
2   Who says they saw these things?
3   Which of these things do you think it would it be possible to see? Which lines are true?
4   Which of these things is it impossible to see? Which lines are not true?
5   Can a peacock have a 'fiery' tail (line 1)? What does 'fiery' mean? What kind of word is it?

6   Could you see the sun even in the midst of night (line 11)? How, or why not?

7   Who do you think the 'man who saw this wondrous sight' could have been?

8   Could a fishpond 'be all on fire' (line 13)?

9   Could a girl be 'just like a cat' (line 21)? If so how, if not why not?

10   What makes this a poem? How does each line link with the next?

Thinking about seeing

Key question: What does seeing mean?

1   How do we see things? How does the eye work?

2   What would it be like if you could not see? What would it be like if you were blind from birth?

3   Can you 'see' in your mind, or in your 'mind's eye'?

4   Can you picture anything, even impossible things, in your mind or 'mind's eye'?

5   Have you ever thought you saw something which was not really there? Give an example.

6   Can you see something and think it is something else? Give an example.

7   Is seeing believing? If you see something do you always believe what you see? Why?

8   Can you see something which you cannot describe?

9   Do you remember everything you see? How do you know?

10   Can you know something without ever having seen it? Give examples.

Further activities

•   Blindfold a child – can s/he identify different objects on a tray without seeing them?

•   Study the workings of the human eye and animal eyes.

•   Brainstorm a thesaurus of 'seeing' words eg glimpse, inspect, view, glance.

•   Investigate eyes of people you know eg chart eye colour, or blinks per minute.

•   Close your eyes and visualise a journey through a favourite scene. Try to imagine 'seeing' something amazing. Draw, paint or describe what you have 'seen'.

Further poems for thinking

Other poems about seeing to read and think about include: 'On His Blindness' by John Milton, 'Thirteen Ways of Looking at a Blackbird' by Wallace Stevens and 'Magic Mirror' by Judith Nicholls.

22

The Strange Wild Song

He thought he saw an Elephant
    That practised on a fife:
He looked again and found it was
    A letter from his wife.
5   'At length I realise,' he said,
    'The bitterness of Life!'

He thought he saw a Buffalo,
    Upon a chimney-piece:
He looked again, and found it was
10   His Sister's Husband's Niece.
'Unless you leave this house,' he said,
    'I'll send for the Police!'

He thought he saw a Rattlesnake,
    That questioned him in Greek;
15 He looked again, and found it was
    The Middle of Next Week.
'The one thing I regret,' he said,
    'Is that it cannot speak!'

He thought he saw a Banker's Clerk
20   Descending from a bus;
He looked again and found it was
    A Hippopotamus.
'If this should stay to dine,' he said,
    'There won't be much for us!'

25 He thought he saw a Kangaroo
    That worked a coffee mill;
He looked again, and found it was
    A Vegetable Pill.
If I were to swallow this,' he said,
30   'I should be very ill!'

> He thought he saw a Coach-and-four
>   That stood beside his bed;
> He looked again and found it was
>   A Bear without a Head;
> 35   'Poor thing,' he said, 'poor silly thing!
>   It's waiting to be fed!'
>
> He thought he saw an Albatross
>   That fluttered round the Lamp;
> He looked again, and found it was,
> 40   A Penny Postage stamp.
> 'You'd best be getting home,' he said,
>   'The nights are very damp!'

Lewis Carroll

Thinking about the poem

Key question: What does the poem mean?

1   This is called a 'Strange Wild Song'. Is there a difference between a poem and a song? Is this a poem or a song?

2   In what ways is is it strange or wild?

3   Do you think what was described in the first verse could happen? Can you explain why?

4   What kind of thing is 'The Middle of Next Week' (line 16)?

5   Is it possible to look at something, then look again and realise it is something else? Has that ever happened to you?

6   What patterns of words can you see in this poem?

7   When do you think this poem was written? Are there any clues in the words of the poem?

8   Some people call this a Nonsense Poem. What do you think they mean by this?

9   What things in this poem are possible, and what are impossible?

10   Does a nonsense poem mean it has no sense at all? Can you make sense of this poem?

Thinking about sense and nonsense

Key question: What is nonsense?

1   What is nonsense? Can you give an example?

2   Can you make up a nonsense word that doesn't mean anything at all?

3   Can you make up a nonsense sentence out of words that make sense?

4   Can things be nonsense to one person and make sense to another?

5   Do you know any poem, song or story that is nonsense? Can you say it?

6   Some things are impossible, and some things seem impossible but might be possible. Are these impossible – a red banana, a square circle, a snake that can talk? Why?

7   What things are impossible? Can you give examples?

8   Can you think of something that seems impossible, but under certain circumstances could happen? Give an example.

9   Are there some things which you are not sure whether to believe or not? Give an example. What would prove it to be true or untrue?

10   Is seeing believing? If you see something can you be sure of what you see?

Further activities

• Write your own nonsense poem.

• List an equal number of examples under three categories: Things I know are ...Certain/Possible/Impossible

• Draw something that is impossible.

• Find and view some optical illusions eg the drawings of Escher. Choose one to draw.

• Make up your own dictionary of nonsense words and their meanings.

Further poems for thinking

Other poems by Lewis Carroll to read and think about include: 'Jabberwocky', 'The White Knight's Song' and 'You are Old Father William'. Other poets who wrote nonsense verse include Edward Lear, Mervyn Peake and Spike Milligan.

23

To Sleep

A flock of sheep that leisurely pass by,
One after one; the sound of rain and bees
Murmuring; the fall of rivers, winds and seas,
Smooth fields, white sheets of water, and pure sky;
5   I have thought of all by turns, and yet do lie
Sleepless! and soon the small birds' melodies
Must hear, first uttered from my orchard trees;
And the first cuckoo's melancholy cry.
Even thus last night, and two nights more, I lay
10 And could not win thee, sleep! by any stealth:
So do not let me wear tonight away:
Without thee what is all the morning's wealth?
Come, blessed barrier between night and day,
Dear mother of fresh thought and joyous health!

William Wordsworth

Who Dreams?

Once Chuang Tzu dreamt he was a butterfly,
fluttering here and there,
aware he was a butterfly.
Suddenly he awoke
5   and found he was Chuang Tzu.

Now he does not know
if he was Chuang Tzu
dreaming he was a butterfly,
or a butterfly
10 dreaming he is Chuang Tzu.

Chuang Tzu, China, translated by Robert Fisher

Thinking about the poems

Key question: What do the poems mean?

1 What does the poet think of when he is trying to go to sleep?
2 What do you think of when trying to go to sleep?
3 Why do you think the poet in the first poem cannot get to sleep?
4 How does he know when morning has come?
5 How many nights has he gone without sleep?
6 How did the poet try to win sleep by 'stealth' (line 10)?
7 What does his question mean: 'Without thee what is all this morning's wealth?' (line 12)?
8 Who dreams in the second poem? How do you know?
9 How are these poems similar? How are they different?
10 Which do you prefer? Why?

Thinking about sleep and dreams

Key question: What do sleep and dreaming mean?

1 Do you know what it feels like to fall asleep? How or why?
2 What is the difference between being awake and being asleep?
3 Why do people sleep? Why do they want to sleep?
4 Do you find it easy to sleep? Why? What helps you to go to sleep?
5 What is the difference between a dream and a daydream?
6 What sort of things do you dream about? Why do you have those kinds of dream?
7 Can you make yourself dream about certain things?
8 How do you know you are awake and not dreaming now? Is it possible everything is a dream?
9 Can you have a dream and not remember it? How do you know you've had a dream?
10 Do you think we can learn anything from our dreams?

Further activities

• Discuss human (and animal) experiences of going to sleep and waking up.
• Write or record people's accounts of their dreams or nightmares.
• Survey and make a graph of the sleeping habits of a group of people you know.
• Listen to some 'sleepy' music eg 'The Cradle Song' by Brahms. Make up a lullaby, and set it to music.

- Write a story about waking up many years from now (eg a modern version of Sleeping Beauty or Rip van Winkle).

Further poems for thinking

Other poems by William Wordsworth to read and think about include: 'Daffodils', 'Upon Westminster Bridge', 'The Rainbow', and parts of 'The Prelude'.

Other poems about sleep include: 'An Attempt to Charm Sleep' by Elizabeth Jennings, 'Falling Asleep' by Siegfried Sassoon, 'Lights Out' by Edward Thomas and 'Waking Up' by Eleanor Farjeon.

24

Who Are You?

I'm Nobody! Who are you?
Are you – Nobody – too?
Then there's a pair of us?
Don't tell! They'd advertise – you know!

How dreary – to be – Somebody!
How public – like a Frog –
To tell one's name – the livelong June –
To an admiring Bog!

Emily Dickinson

Somebody

Somebody being a nobody,
Thinking to look like a somebody,
Said he thought me a nobody:
Good little somebody-nobody,
Had you not known me a somebody,
Would you have called me a nobody?

Alfred, Lord Tennyson

Mr Nobody

I know a funny little man,
  As quiet as a mouse,
Who does the mischief that is done
  In everybody's house!
There's no one ever sees his face,
  And yet we all agree
That every plate we break was cracked
  By Mr Nobody.

Anon (first verse of the poem)

Thinking about the poems

Key question: What do the poems mean?

1   In Emily Dickinson's poem, who do you think she is talking to?
2   Why does she say she is a Nobody?
3   Why does she not want to be a Somebody?
4   Who or what do you think 'an admiring Bog' is?
5   In Tennyson's poem, why do you think somebody said he thought he was a nobody?
6   Why does Tennyson call him a 'somebody-nobody'? What does he mean by this?
7   What kind of somebody was Tennyson?
8   Why do you think Tennyson wrote this poem?
9   Who wrote the poem 'Mr Nobody'?
10   Which do you think is the best poem? Which poem do you like best? Why?

Thinking about somebody and nobody

Key question: What does being somebody and nobody mean?

1   What does it mean to be somebody? Is it different from being a somebody?
2   What does it mean to be nobody? Is it different from being a nobody?
3   Do all things belong to somebody?
4   What things belong to you?
5   Do some things belong to everybody? Can you give any examples?
6   What things belong to nobody? Can you give any examples?
7   If something is nobody's does it mean it is anybody's?
8   Would you prefer to be a somebody or a nobody? Why?
9   If you had no name how would you refer to yourself?
10   Are you nobody, somebody, everybody, or anybody? Why do you think so?

Further activities

- Brainstorm words to fit under four columns – Nobody's, Everybody's, Somebody's and Anybody's.
- Write a poem or short story including the words – nobody, somebody, anybody, and everybody.
- Describe somebody in the room without saying their name, and see who can guess who it is first.
- Choose somebody to be, other than yourself. Make up your life story as this person. Write, describe or be interviewed about your life as this person.
- Play 'Mystery Voices' (see Games for Thinking p 45).

Further poems for thinking

Other poems by Emily Dickinson to read and think about include: 'The Grass', 'A Book', 'In This Short Life' and 'Pedigree'.

25

All the World's a Stage

All the world's a stage
And all the men and women merely players:
They have their exits and their entrances;
And one man in his time plays many parts,
His acts being seven ages. At first the infant,
Mewling and puking in his nurse's arms.
Then the whining schoolboy, with his satchel
And shining morning face, creeping like snail
Unwillingly to school. And then the lover
Sighing like furnace, with a woeful ballad
Made to his mistress' eyebrow. Then a soldier,
Full of strange oaths, and bearded like the pard,
Jealous in honour, sudden and quick in quarrel,
Seeking the bubble reputation
Even in the cannon's mouth. And then the justice,
In fair round belly with good capon lined,
With eyes severe and beard of formal cut,
Full of wise saws and modern instances;
And so he plays his part. The sixth age shifts
Into the lean and slippered pantaloon,
With spectacles on nose and pouch on side,
His youthful hose, well saved, a world too wide
For his shrunk shank; and his big manly voice,
Turning again towards childish treble, pipes
And whistles in his sound. Last scene of all,
That ends this strange eventful history,
Is second childishness and mere oblivion,
Sans teeth, sans eyes, sans taste, sans everything.

William Shakespeare
(from *As You Like It*, Act 2, Scene 7)

pard = leopard
sans = without

Thinking about the poem

Key question: What does the poem mean?

1   In what way is the world is like a stage? How is living like being in a play?

2   Are there any ways in which men and women are like players or actors?

3   What are the seven parts or ages that Shakespeare says 'one man in his time plays'?

4   Which of Shakespeare's seven ages are you most like?

5   Do you, or did you, 'creep like snail unwillingly to school' (lines 8/9)?

6   What is a 'woeful ballad' (line 10)? Why might someone in love sigh and be 'woeful'?

7   What does Shakespeare say a soldier is like?

8   What does Shakespeare say happens to people in old age?

9   Shakespeare says the last scene 'is second childishness'. Are there ways in which very old people might be like children?

10   This writing by Shakespeare comes from one of his plays. Is it a poem? Why?

Thinking about time

Key question: What does growing older mean?

1   How old will you be when you are grown up?

2   Does everyone grow up at the same time? What is the difference between growing up and being old?

3   Could a person be old and young at the same time?

4   As you get older are you always changing? What changes? What stays the same?

5   Do you like your present age? Would you like to be older, or younger, or your age? Why?

6   Are there different stages in life from birth to death? What are they?

7   What does it mean to be old? How are the old different from the young?

8   Are you as old as you feel, or old as you look? How do you know you are as old as you are?

9   What is the best age to be? Is it better to be old or young? Why?

10   Can people of different ages understand each other?

Further activities

- Collect pictures of people eg cut from magazines. Sort them into sets according to what age or stage of life they are. Discuss your criteria for selection.
- Do a close observational drawing of a baby and/or very old person.
- Draw or paint pictures of each stage of life described in Shakespeare's poem.
- Mime one of the stages of life in Shakespeare's poem. Can others guess which one?
- Write your own poem or description about the stages of life.

Further poems for thinking

Other poems by Shakespeare to read and think about include: 'Fear no more the heat o' the sun' (*Cymbeline* Act 4, Scene 2), 'Blow, blow thou winter wind' (*As You Like It*, Act 2, Scene 7), 'Crabbed age and youth' (*The Passionate Pilgrim*, 12).

Other poems about growing old to think about include: 'You are old, Father William' by Lewis Carroll, 'When I am Old' by Jenny Joseph and 'Old People' by Elizabeth Jennings.

26

The Mountain and the Squirrel

The mountain and the squirrel
Had a quarrel;
And the former called the latter 'Little Prig.'
Bun replied,
5   You are doubtless very big;
But all sorts of things and weather
Must be taken together,
To make up a year
And a sphere.
10 And I think it no disgrace
To occupy my place.
If I'm not so large as you,
You are not so small as I,
And not half so spry,
15 I'll not deny you make
A very pretty squirrel track;
Talents differ; all is well and wisely put;
If I cannot carry forests on my back,
Neither can you crack a nut.'

Ralph Waldo Emerson

Thinking about the poem

Key question: What does the poem mean?

1   Ralph Waldo Emerson called this poem 'A Fable.' What is a fable? Why is it like a fable?

2   What is a 'prig'? Why do you think the mountain called the squirrel 'Little Prig'?

3   Who was 'Bun'? Why do you think he or she is called 'Bun' in the poem?

4   What does the poem say makes up a year and a sphere?

5   In what ways does the squirrel compare him or herself to the mountain?

6   What do you think 'is well and wisely put' (line 17)?

7   What do you think the mountain might say to the squirrel?

8   Would you rather be a mountain or a squirrel? Why?

9   Do you know any other fables? Who wrote fables? What is the moral of this fable?

10   Why are the lines of the poem so short? What makes this a poem?

Thinking about talents

Key question: What does talent mean?

1   What is a talent?

2   What are you good at doing? How do you know?

3   What are you not good at doing? How do you know?

4   Is everyone good at something? Are some things better to be good at than others? Why?

5   What kind of world would it be if everyone was good at everything?

6   What kind of world would it be if no-one was good at anything?

7   Do you know how good you are at everything?

8   Do you think you get better at things as you get older? Do you get better at thinking?

9   How do you get better at something you want to be good at? Can you give an example?

10   Do you think some people don't know how good or talented they are? If so, why might this be?

Further activities

- Read and discuss The Parable of the Talents (Matthew 25, 14-30 in the Bible).
- Hold a Talent Show, where everyone is invited to either show, tell, sing, dance, act, mime, or play a musical instrument etc.
- Invite a talented artist, sportsperson or musician to talk or be interviewed about their special talent and how it has been developed.
- Write your own fable between two animal characters, one of whom thinks they are much cleverer than the other.
- Write a list or poem about My Talents or What I Can Do.

Further poems for thinking

Other poems by Emerson to read and think about include: 'The Past', 'Music' and 'Hamatreya'.

27

Parrot

Sometimes I sit with both eyes closed,
But all the same, I've heard:
They're saying, 'He won't talk because
He is a *thinking* bird.'

5   I'm olive green and sulky, and
The family say, 'Oh yes,
He's silent, but he's *listening*,
He *thinks* more than he says!

'He ponders on the things he hears,
10   Preferring not to chatter.'
– And this is true, but *why* it's true
Is quite another matter.

I'm working out some shocking things
In order to surprise them,
15   And when my thoughts are ready I'll
Certainly *not* disguise them!

I'll wait, and see, and choose a time
When everyone is present,
And clear my throat and raise my beak
20   And give a squawk and start to speak
And go on for about a week
And it will not be pleasant!

Alan Brownjohn

Thinking about the poem

Key question: What does the poem mean?

1 Why do you think the parrot sometimes sits with both eyes closed?
2 Why do you think the parrot won't talk?
3 How does the parrot describe himself?
4 Why do the family say about the parrot 'He thinks more than he says' (line 8)?
5 What does it mean to 'ponder' (line 9)?
6 What kinds of 'shocking things' do you think the parrot is working out to say?

7 The parrot says he is not going to 'disguise' his thoughts (line 16). How do people disguise their thoughts in what they say? Can you give an example?

8 Why do you think he wants to speak 'for about a week' to say 'what will not be pleasant'?

9 How would you describe the character of the parrot?

10 In what ways is the parrot like and unlike you?

Thinking about thinking

Key question: What does thinking mean?

1 When you think, do you always put your thoughts into words?

2 Can you think without anyone knowing you are thinking? Do you know when other people are thinking? Give an example.

3 Does it help to close your eyes when you think?

4 Would you call yourself a thinking person? Why?

5 What do you think about? What do you think about most? What do you never think about?

6 Do you think more than you say? What do you think that you do not say?

7 Do you think when you are asleep?

8 Is it always a good thing to tell people what you are thinking? When is it? When isn't it?

9 Where do you do your best thinking? Do you think best by yourself or with other people?

10 Do you get better at thinking as you get older? Why?

Further activities

• Draw yourself (or the parrot) thinking and show in your drawing what the thought is like.

• Start a 'Think Book' to write about what you think and learn each day.

• Do a mind-map. Write the word THINKING on the middle of a large page. Write all the words connected to thinking you can think of eg imagine, know, remember, believe etc.

• Draw the inside of your mind or brain to show where thoughts come from. Explain your drawing to others (see *Teaching Children to Think* by Robert Fisher for some brain drawings).

• Write a story about a pet who thought a lot and one day began to talk!

Further poems for thinking

Other poems by Alan Brownjohn to read and think about include: 'The Rabbit' (after Prévert), 'Chameleon', and 'Explorer'.

28

Ozymandias

I met a traveller from an antique land
Who said: Two vast and trunkless legs of stone
Stand in the desert. ... Near them, on the sand,
Half sunk, a shatter'd visage lies, whose frown
5   And wrinkled lip, and sneer of cold command,
Tell that the sculptor well those passions read
Which yet survive, stamped on these lifeless things,
The hand that mocked them and the heart that fed;
And on the pedestal these words appear:
10   'My name is Ozymandias, king of kings:
Look on my works, ye Mighty, and despair!'
Nothing beside remains. Round the decay
Of that colossal wreck, boundless and bare,
The lone and level sands stretch far away.

Percy Bysshe Shelley

Long After Humankind Has Gone

Long after humankind has gone
and cities lie empty
and the sound of machines
is stopped
5   in dark holes there will be life
lying in cracks in the burnt earth
the white seeds of eggs
through the blowing dust come
scuttling legs

10   of animal life
they were the first
in some form they will be
the last of things
long after human hopes are lost
15   when the green world dies
once more life will rise
on tiny wings

Robert Fisher

Thinking about the poem 'Ozymandias'

Key question: What does the poem mean?

1   Where do you think the traveller had come from? Where do you think he had travelled?

2   What is an 'antique land'? What does 'antique' mean?

3   What did the traveller find in the desert?

4   What do we know about Ozymandias? Who do you think he was?

5   What did the traveller mean by saying 'its sculptor well those passions read' (line 6)?

6   What was 'the hand that mocked them', and 'the heart that fed' (line 8)?

7   What were the words on the pedestal? Why were they written?

8   How big do you think 'that colossal wreck' might have been? Why was it a 'wreck'?

9   What does the poem tell us about the past and the passing of time?

10   Is the poem only about the past?

Thinking about time

Key question: What does past and future mean?

1   How do we know about the past?

2   What is time? How do we measure time? Can you have time without a clock?

3   Is time the way things change, or the rate things change?

4   Does everything change with time? Are there some things which do not change?

5   Does time pass quickly, or go slow, or does it have different speeds?

6   If the past is everything up to the present, and the future is everything from the present on, what is the present? How long is the present?

7   Can we go back and live in the past? What time in the past would you like to visit? Why?

8   Can we go and live in the future? What time in the future would you like to visit? Why?

9   Could there be a time machine in which you could travel back or forward in time?

10   How will the future be similar to or different from the present?

Further activities

- Collect and display artefacts that mark the passing of time – lock, watch, hour glass, sundial, egg-timer, metronome etc.

- Create a time-line charting the major events of your life and also the public events that have taken place during your life. Continue the time line into the future.

- Draw the place where you are, how you think it might have looked long ago. Draw it as it might be a long time into the future. Discuss and compare your drawings.

- Model your own version of the statue of Ozymandias out of clay. First sketch your design.

- Choose and discuss ten things you would put in a Time Capsule to tell people in the future what life was like now.

Further poems for thinking

Other poems by Shelley to read and think about include: 'Evening: Ponte al Mare, Pisa'; 'To Jane: the Invitation' and 'Song'.

Other poems about time to think about include: 'All That's Past' by Walter de la Mare, 'Time, You Old Gipsy Man' by Ralph Hodgson and 'Egypt's Might is Tumbled Down' by Mary Coleridge.

29

These I Have Loved

These I have loved:
    White plates and cups, clean-gleaming,
Ringed with blue lines; and feathery, faery dust;
Wet roofs, beneath the lamp-light; the strong crust
5   Of friendly bread; and many tasting food;
Rainbows; and the blue bitter smoke of wood;
And radiant raindrops couching in cool flowers;
And flowers themselves, that sway through sunny hours,
Dreaming of moths that drink them under the moon;
10 Then, the cool kindliness of sheets, that soon
Smooth away trouble; and the rough male kiss
Of blankets; grainy wood; live hair that is
Shining and free; blue massing clouds; the keen
Unpassioned beauty of a great machine;
15 The benison of hot water; furs to touch;
The good smell of old clothes; and other such –
The comfortable smell of friendly fingers,
Hair's fragrance, and the musty reek that lingers
About dead leaves and last year's ferns ...
20   Dear names,
And thousand other throng to me! Royal flames;
Sweet water's dimpling laugh from tap to spring;
Holes in the ground; and voices that do sing;
Voices in laughter, too; and body's pain,
25 Soon turned to peace; and the deep-panting train;
Firm sands; the little dulling edge of foam
That browns and dwindles as the wave goes home;
And washen stones, gay for an hour; the cold
Graveness of iron; moist black earthen mould;
30 Sleep; and high places; footprints in the dew;
And oaks; and brown horse-chestnuts glossy-new;
And new-peeled sticks; and shining pools on grass; –
All these have been my loves ...

Rupert Brooke (from 'The Great Lover')

Thinking about the poem

Key question: What does the poem mean?

1 When the poet says 'These I have loved ...', is he speaking about the past or the present?

2 Which of the things the poet mentions do you like?

3 Which of them, if any, do you love?

4 Which of them, if any, do you not like?

5 Are there any words in this poem you do not understand? If so, can you guess what they might mean?

6 What does the 'benison' of hot water mean (line 15)? What is water's 'dimpling laugh' (line 22)?

7 Which words relate to the sense of sight, of sound, of smell, of taste and of touch?

8 When the poet mentions 'Dear names' (line 20), what do you think he is thinking of?

9 Is this a poem about what the poet is thinking or what he is feeling?

10 What makes this writing a poem?

Thinking about treasures

Key question: What does loving things mean?

1 What things in your life do you love most? Do you own the things you love?

2 Do you have one special treasure? What would you save if you could save just one thing that you own?

3 What would you say was the most precious thing in the world? Why is it so precious?

4 What is your favourite sight, sound, smell, taste and thing to touch?

5 Can you think of a fairy story or folk tale about finding treasure? Why are so many stories about finding treasure of some kind?

6 What is your 'pot of gold at the end of a rainbow' (what thing in the world do you most wish for)? Why?

7 If you found a hidden treasure who would it belong to?

8 Do you have something you love which is of no value at all?

9 Is there someone you would describe as a 'treasure'?

10 Is it good to treasure things in life? Why?

Further activities

- Display treasures of real or sentimental value in a careful setting.
- Research the golden treasures of peoples such as the Egyptians, Greeks and Incas.
- Act the ancient Greek legend of King Midas and the Golden Touch.
- Write a story about a map showing lost treasure, and illustrate it with a treasure map.
- Write a poem listing and describing the things you love or like the most.

Further poems for thinking

Other poems by Rupert Brooke to read and think about include: 'Heaven' and 'The Soldier'.

Other poems about sensory delights include 'Pleasant Sounds' by John Clare.

30

The False Knight upon the Road

'O where are you going?'
   Said the false knight upon the road.
'I'm going to school,'
   Said the small boy, and still he stood.

5   'What's that on your back?'
   Said the false knight on the road.
'My books, can't you see?'
   Said the small boy, and still he stood.

'What's that under your arm?'
10   *Said the false knight on the road.*
'Coal for the school fire, can't you see?'
   Said the small boy, and still he stood.

'Who owns those sheep?'
   Said the false knight on the road.
15   'They're mine and my mother's,'
   Said the small boy, and still he stood.

'How many of them are mine?'
   Said the false knight on the road.
'All those with blue tails,'
20   *Said the small boy, and still he stood.*

'I wish you were on that tree over there,'
   Said the false knight on the road.
'And a good ladder under me,'
   Said the small boy, and still he stood.

25   'And the ladder would break.'
   Said the false knight on the road.
'And you'd fall down,'
   Said the small boy, and still he stood.

'I wish you were in the sea,'
30   *Said the false knight on the road.*
'And a good ship under me,'
   Said the small boy, and still he stood.

'And the ship would break,'
Said the false knight on the road.
35   'And you be drowned,'
Said the small boy, and still he stood.

Anon

Thinking about the poem

Key question: What does the poem mean?

1   Who do you think the 'false knight' was?
2   Why do you think he was called 'false'?
3   Why do you think he was there 'on the road'?
4   What do we know from the poem about the small boy?
5   Why did the false knight question the small boy?
6   What was the strangest question the false knight asked the small boy?
7   What do you think was the best answer given by the small boy? Why?
8   What do you think happened after the poem ends?
9   What makes this a poem? Wy are some lines in italics?
10   Who do you think wrote the poem? Why do you think they wrote it?

Thinking about truth

Key question: What do true and false mean?

1   When is something false? Can you give an example?
2   Can you think of another word or words that mean something similar to false?
3   Can people be false? Give an example.
4   Are false teeth really false? Is a copy of something false?
5   Can you be false to yourself? If so, how? If not, why not?
6   Could something be false and true at the same time? Can you say why?
7   Have you ever believed something that was false was true? Give an example.
8   Is fiction always false? Is a fact always true?
9   Could you have a world where everything was false?
10   What is the difference between believing something is true (or false) and knowing it is true (or false)?

Further activities

- Collect and display as many 'false' or reproduction items as you can eg wigs, false teeth, moustaches etc.

- Design and create your own lifelike but 'false' object eg flower, fried egg, insect.

- Make up a poem, story or play about a child being stopped by a 'false' stranger and the conversation they have, showing how the child outwits the stranger.

- Play a game of telling 'tall stories'. Each player takes turns in telling a story. Others must guess whether the story is true or false (ie a 'tall story').

- Read and discuss the story 'Not true!' (in *Stories for Thinking* p 106).

Further poems for thinking

Other anonymous ballads about the true and the false to read and think about include: 'Edward Edward', 'Thomas Rhymer', 'The Outlandish Knight', and 'King John and the Abbott of Canterbury'.

31

Vocation

When the gong sounds ten in the morning and I walk to school by our lane,
   Every day I meet the hawker crying, 'Bangles, crystal bangles!'
   There is nothing to hurry him on, there is no road he must take, no place he must go to, no time when he must come home,
5   I wish I were a hawker, spending my day on the road, crying, 'Bangles, crystal bangles!'

When at four in the afternoon I come back from the school,
   I can see through the gate of that house the gardener digging the ground.
   He does what he likes with his spade, he soils his clothes with dust,
10   nobody takes him to task if he gets baked in the sun or gets wet.
   I wish I were a gardener digging away at the garden with nobody to stop me from digging.

Just as it gets dark in the evening and my mother sends me to bed,
   I can see through my open window the watchman walking up and down.
15   The lane is dark and lonely, and the street-lamp stands like a giant with one red eye in its head.
   The watchman swings his lantern and walks with his shadow at his side, and never once goes to bed in his life.
   I wish I were a watchman walking the street all night, chasing
20   the shadows with my lantern.

Rabindranath Tagore

Thinking about the poem

Key question: What does the poem mean?

1   Do you know what the title 'Vocation' means? What do you think it means?

2   Is the poem set in this country, or another country? Why do you think so?

3   What sounds does the poet hear in the first verse? Where are they coming from?

4   Why does the poet want to be a hawker?

5   Where does he see a gardener?

6   Why does he want to be a gardener?

7   What sights can he see through his bedroom window?

8   Why does he want to be a watchman?

9   Would you rather be a hawker, gardener or watchman? Why?

10 Was the person who wrote this poem a child? What are your reasons for thinking this?

Thinking about work

Key question: What does vocation mean?

1   Do you work? What work do you do? What is your most important work?

2   Does everyone do a job of work? Why, or why not?

3   Is staying at home and looking after a house a job of work?

4   What work would you like to do when you grow up? Why?

5   Do you prefer to work with others or by yourself? Why?

6   What is the difference between work and play?

7   Can play be hard work? Can work be like play? Give examples.

8   Do people work to help themselves or to help other people? Do you work to help other people?

9   Do you think people only work for money?

10 What do you think are the most important jobs of work in society?

Further activities

- List all the categories of work you can think of. Write examples under each category.
- Research and chart the jobs people in your group or class want to do when they grow up.
- Make up a work song for work you have to do.
- Take turns to mime other people's jobs. Can people guess the job ('What's my line')?
- Interview someone for whom work is a vocation eg charity aid worker, nurse, priest.

Further poems for thinking

Other poems by Rabindranath Tagore to read and think about include: 'Highest Price', 'Paper Boats' and 'Fairyland'.

32

The Magic Box

I will put into the box

the swish of a silk sari on a summer night,
fire from the nostrils of a Chinese dragon,
the tip of a tongue touching a tooth.

5   I will put into the box

a snowman with a rumbling belly,
a sip of the bluest water from Lake Lucerne,
a leaping spark from an electric fish.

I will put into the box

10   three violet wishes spoken in Gujarati,
the last joke of an ancient uncle
and the first smile of a baby.

I will put in the box

a fifth season and a black sun,
15   a cowboy on a broomstick
and a witch on a white horse.

My box is fashioned from ice and gold and steel,
with stars on the lid and secrets in the corners.
Its hinges are the toe joints
20   of dinosaurs.

I shall surf in my box
on the great high-rolling breakers of the wild Atlantic,
then wash ashore on a yellow beach
the colour of the sun.

Kit Wright

Thinking about the poem

Key question: What does the poem mean?

1   The poem is called 'The Magic Box'. Is the poem about magic?
2   What kind of box is it?
3   The poem mentions things from many parts of the world. What different countries do the things put in the box come from?
4   Which is your favourite line in the poem (or favourite thing put into the box)?
5   Which of the things put in the box are real, and which unreal or imaginary?
6   What do you think is the strangest thing put in the box? What is strange about it?
7   Can you describe how the box is made?
8   What does the poet want to do in the box? Why?
9   What makes this a poem? What is special about the way it is written?
10   What do you like, or not like, about this poem?

Thinking about wishes

Key question: What does it mean to make a wish?

1   What happens in your mind when you make a wish?
2   Do you think everyone has wishes? What do people wish for?
3   Do wishes come true? Have any of your wishes come true? Give an example.
4   Does wishing for something help it happen?
5   What one thing do you wish for most? Can you help your wish to come true?
6   What things do you not wish for? Who are your wishes addressed to?
7   Is wishing the same as wanting? Is wishing the same as hoping? Is wishing the same as begging?
8   Do you know any stories about wishes? Why in fairy stories are there always three wishes?
9   Are there any occasions when you make a wish? When might you make a wish? Why?
10   Is it a good thing for people to have everything they wish for? Why?

Further activities

- Write a story about a wish that came true, with unexpected consequences.
- Draw a picture or poster showing your wishes for the world.
- Make a silent wish and mime it to others. Can they guess what your wish is?
- Write a poem about wishes eg your own magic box of wishes (modelled on the poem) or one with lines beginning 'I wish I could live/play/read/visit/see/hear/smell/feel …'.
- Design your own magic box of wishes, make it and invite people to put their wishes in it.

Further poems for thinking

Other poems by Kit Wright to read and think about include: 'Every Day in Every Way', 'The Frozen Man' and 'Lies'.

Glossary of terms

acrostic poem	A poem in which the initial letters of each line make a word or words when read downwards.
alliteration	The repetition of initial letters in words either next to or near to each other, as in 'makes much of a miracle'.
anthology	A collection of poems or passages of writing, often with a unifying theme.
assonance	The repetition of similar vowel sounds close to each other, to achieve a particular kind of word music or rhyme.
ballad	A poem or song which tells a story. The traditional ballad was an anonymous folk ballad characterised by short verses and simple words, such as 'The False Knight upon the Road' (p 99). Literary ballads were written in the 19th and 20th centuries, such as Tennyson's 'Lady of Shalott'. The word ballad today also refers to songs of love.
blank verse	Poetry written in *iambic pentameters* (five stress lines), without rhymes. Most of Shakespeare's plays are written in blank verse.
carol	A form of song often sung at Christmas which originated in France as a kind of round dance.
cinquain	A poetic form invented by American poet Adelaide Crapsey with the following syllabic line count: 2, 4, 6, 8, 2.
cliché	Language that has become stale and commonplace through repetition.
collage poem	A poem that has been put together from lines, sentences or phrases from other sources.
consonance	The repetition of the same consonant in words close to each other.
couplet	Two adjacent lines of the same metre which rhyme.

dialect	A way of speaking or writing that is special to a locality or social group.
draft	A rough plan, outline or working version of a piece of writing.
elegy	A sad poem or lament about the death of a particular person.
epic	A long poem, usually about a heroic adventure. Traditional epics include *Beowulf*, and the *Iliad* and *Odyssey* of Homer.
epigram	A short, neat and often witty saying.
epitaph	An inscription that is or could be written on a tombstone.
eye rhyme or sight rhyme	A pair of syllables which look as though they should rhyme but do not, for example 'love' and 'move'.
fantasy	Strange, imaginative and non-realistic kinds of thinking or writing.
first person	Speaking or writing using the 'I' voice.
form or format	The physical appearance of a poem on the page in terms of size or line arrangement. Poems are either free form and could be written down in different ways, or are fixed form such as *sonnet, cinquain,* and *villanelle*.
found poem	A poem that has not been deliberately composed but has been found by chance in another context, for example as part of an advert.
free association	A spontaneous connecting of images and ideas.
free verse	Poetry that does not use a traditional rhyming pattern.
haiku	Originally a short Japanese poem of three lines with the syllabic count of 5, 7, 5 and with the first and third lines rhyming.
half-rhyme	A rhyme that does not rhyme fully, but only partially eg 'Beanz meanz - Heinz.'
iambic pentameter	A line with five stressed syllables. English poets have used the iambic line for poetry since the time of Chaucer. Most ballads, songs, hymns and poems have been written in it.

imagery	Vivid description of a visible object or scene so that we can see or sense what is being written about.
kenning	An Old English poetic convention in which one object is represented by another which is associated with it, for example 'whale's road' meaning 'sea'.
limerick	A comic or nonsense poem writen in five lines, using the rhyming scheme AABBA, in which the third and fourth lines are shorter than the rest.
lyric	Originally in Greek 'of the lyre'. Later used about any short poem which expresses a strong feeling or mood. Now used to refer to the words of a song.
metaphor	A type of figurative language in which one thing is described in terms of another thing eg 'All the world's a stage' (p 86). Metaphors, since Aristotle, have been seen as the most distinctive type of poetic language. A whole poem can be an extended metaphor.
metre	Means 'measure', and refers to the regular rhythms of stressed and unstressed syllables in poetry.
narrative poem	A poem that tells a story or narrates a series of events.
nonsense verse	Verse that for funny or playful reasons does not make obvious sense.
ode	A poem expressing strong feeling that is longer and more complex than a lyric.
onomatopoeia	A word whose sound imitates its meaning eg dong, ping, whizz, zoom.
oral tradition	Traditional stories, songs and poems handed down by word of mouth from one generation to another.
palindrome	A poem or sentence which reads the same backwards or torwards.
parable	A short story or poem which has a hidden moral or spiritual meaning.
parody	To imitate a piece of writing, usually to make fun of the original.
pastoral	A form of writing derived from ancient Greek and Latin literature in which the countryside and its people are celebrated.

personification	Presenting an object or idea as a person with human qualities or feelings.
prose poem	Writing written as prose but with the sound quality and compression of poetry.
quatrain	The most common stanza in English poetry, consisting of four lines, usually rhymed.
rap	Rhythmic spoken poetry, sometimes set to music, which probably originated in street carnivals in the West Indies.
refrain	A phrase or verse which recurs at intervals, especially at the end of each stanza of a poem or song.
renga	A series of *haiku* linked by a common theme.
rhyme	Words or final syllables in words which sound identical or very similar, usually occurring at the ends of lines of verse. A rhyme may be one syllable (house/mouse), two syllable (looking/cooking) or three syllables (bicycle/tricycle). A rhyme scheme is the pattern of rhyming sounds that occur in a poem. These are usually indicated by letters of the alphabet eg ABAB.
rhythm	The pattern of stressed and unstressed syllables in speech. In poetry the rhythmic unit is called the metre or measure.
run-on line	Lines in which the meaning and syntax lead you on to the next line eg 'It's funny how the things you're told/Can never lead to pots of gold.'
scansion	The analysis of the metrical pattern of a poem.
shape poem	A poem written in the shape of an object.
simile	The direct comparison of one thing with another, generally connected with 'as' or 'like' eg 'pure as a pearl' (p 25).
sonnet	A fixed form of poem, generally fourteen lines, using iambic pentameter (five stresses per line).
stanza	The group of lines in which a poem is divided.
stress	That part of a word or syllable on which the emphasis falls when spoken. Stress can be loudness, raised pitch or length of syllable. Stress is a feature of all English speech. In poetry it creates rhythm.
surreal	Something which seems dreamlike or absurd.

syllable	The smallest unit of English speech sound (phoneme). A syllable must include a central vowel (some words like 'I', 'a' and 'oh' contain no more than this). Some words are one syllable eg 'tree' and others are multisyllabic. The way syllables are stressed or unstressed creates the rhythms of speech and poetry. Some poems such as haiku and cinquains have a set number of syllables.
symbol	A particular type of sign where an object represents another object, relationship or idea, for example a dove may represent peace.
theme	The main idea of a poem, or what the poem is about. A poem may have a number of themes.
tone	The attitude suggested by the voice of the poem eg humorous, sad, lonely, gentle, angry.
villanelle	A fixed form of poem, containing 19 lines, with five three-line stanzas and a final four line stanza.

Index of poets

William Blake
(1757-1827)

English poet and painter who often illustrated his own poems. His books of poems include *Songs of Innocence* (1789) and *Songs of Experience* (1794). His most famous poem 'Jerusalem' ends: 'I will not cease from Mental Fight,/Nor shall my Sword sleep in my hand,/Till we have built Jerusalem/In England's green and pleasant Land.'

James Berry
(born 1924)

One of the best known Caribbean poets. He was born in Jamaica, but moved to England in 1948. He has written many books of poetry for both children and adults including *When I Dance* and *Hot Earth, Cold Earth*. In 1990 he was awarded an OBE for his poetry and for his work in support of black writers.

Rupert Brooke
(1887-1915)

English poet who died in Greece during the First World War. He was a favourite poet among young people during the 1920s and 1930s. His most famous poem is a sonnet called 'The Soldier', about his thoughts as a soldier in the First World War.

Alan Brownjohn
(born 1931)

Modern English poet. He has written many poems about animals, his best known being 'The Rabbit' , about people going to see the last rabbit in England. It also has the title 'After Prévert', as it was written in the style of the French poet Jacques Prévert.

Lewis Carroll
(1832-1898)

Victorian English writer and mathematician whose real name was Charles Ludwidge Dodgson. He wrote *Alice's Adventures in Wonderland* (1865), and *Through the Looking Glass* (1872) which includes his famous nonsense poem 'Jabberwocky'. These books have been translated into every major language of the world.

Walter de la Mare
(1873-1956)

English poet who wrote for adults and children. His poems often have a sense of mystery and magic, like 'Someone', which begins: 'Some one came knocking/At my wee small door;/ Someone came knocking,/I'm sure – sure – sure;/I listened, I opened,/I looked to left and right,/But nought was there a-stirring/In the still dark night.'

Emily Dickinson (1830-1886)	American poet who lived all her life in her family home, never married and wrote in secret more than 1000 poems. When these were published after her death she became famous. Many of her short poems are about what she saw and thought, and pose questions to the reader such as: 'In this short Life/That only lasts an hour/How much – how little is/Within our power.'
Ralph Waldo Emerson (1803-1882)	Famous American poet and philosopher of the nineteenth century. One of his best known poems, 'Hamatreya', is about men who boast about the land they own, and one who 'sees not Death, who adds/Him to his land, a lump of mold the more.'
Eleanor Farjeon (1881-1965)	English poet who wrote her first poems at the age of six and continued writing poems all her life. She wrote the words of the hymn 'Morning has Broken' and many rhymes for young children. She said that all her poems were songs that she had sung in her head, and never went anywhere without a pencil and paper to write down ideas.
Robert Fisher (born 1943)	English teacher and writer, who has edited the following poetry anthologies published by Faber: *Amazing Monsters, Ghosts Galore, Funny Folk, Witch Words, Pet Poems*, and *Minibeasts*. He has written many books, including *Stories for Thinking* and *Games for Thinking* in this series.
Robert Frost (1874-1963)	One of the best known American poets of the twentieth century. Most of his poems are about nature and life in New England. He was the favourite poet of President Kennedy who invited him to read his poems at the White House. One of his best-known poems, 'Stopping by Woods on a Snowy Evening', ends: The woods are lovely, dark and deep,/But I have promises to keep,/And miles to go before I sleep,/And miles to go before I sleep.'
Miroslav Holub (born 1923)	Czech poet and scientist who writes in free verse, without rhymes. His use of simple words and images make his poems easy to translate. More of his poems have been translated into English than any other Czech poet. His poem 'The Door' begins: 'Go and open the door./Maybe outside there is/a tree, or a wood/a garden,/or a magic city ...'

Elizabeth Jennings (born 1926)	Modern English poet who believes the best way to become a poet is to read a lot of poetry. Many of her poems are about love, friendship and family relationships such as 'The Secret Brother'. She wrote poetry she says as 'another way of finding out what life and the world meant.'
Henry Longfellow (1807-1882)	American poet whose most famous poem 'Hiawatha' (1855) was based on tales of native American peoples who in those days were known as Redskins. 'Hiawatha' became one of the most famous poems ever written, owing to its rhythm and simple story. He wrote many narrative poems including 'Paul Revere's Ride', and 'The Skeleton in Armour'.
Roger McGough (born 1937)	Modern English poet, one of today's most popular poets for adults and children, and well known for his public performances of poetry. His poetry books include *Sky in the Pie, Nailing the Shadow* and *You Tell Me* (with Michael Rosen). He believes that poetry is best spoken aloud. He is one of a famous group of poets called the Mersey Poets from Liverpool.
Adrian Mitchell (born 1932)	English writer of poems and plays. He writes about people, places and things. His poems like his rap 'Back in the Playground Blues' (p 27), and 'Dumb Insolence' are about the problems people face. His poem 'Watch Your Step, I'm Drenched' is about rain in Manchester. His poem 'I like that stuff' is about the everyday things he loves.
Christina Rosetti (1830-1894)	English Victorian poet, sister of the poet and painter Dante Gabriel Rossetti. She wrote a famous fantasy poem called 'Goblin Market', and the words for the Christmas carol 'In the Bleak Mid-Winter'. Her poems often express her feelings and her questions about the world, as in 'Who has Seen the Wind?'
Carl Sandburg (1878-1967)	American poet who wrote poems about people, their stories and problems in free verse. His long poem *The People, Yes* includes many smaller poems such as 'What Kind of Liar Are You?' and 'Who Do You Think You Are?' (p 48)

Chief Seattle
(19th century)

Chief Seattle was the native American leader of one of the Northwest Indian Nations in the nineteenth century. He achieved fame through the powerful message he sent to the government in Washington who wanted to buy his people's land. His words were spoken, and translated into written English by an American doctor. They come from a long tradition where poetry, myth, songs and stories are spoken, remembered and handed down from one generation to another.

William Shakespeare
(1564-1616)

English poet and playwright born on April 23rd, St George's Day, 1564, in Stratford-upon-Avon. He died, also on April 23rd, in 1616. He wrote plays which were performed at the Globe Theatre in London. His most famous poems were written as sonnets to a mysterious lady. His plays are written in a form of poetry called blank verse, which are iambic pentamaters without rhymes (as in p 86).

Percy Bysshe Shelley
(1792-1822)

English poet who died aged thirty when he drowned in Italy. He loved freedom and beauty, and wished for a world where people would be free from kings (like Ozymandias), and find beauty in nature, as in the poem 'Evening: Ponte al Mare, Pisa' in which he describes the beauty he sees from a bridge in Italy shortly before he died.

Rabindranath Tagore
(1861-1941)

Indian poet and philosopher who received the Nobel Prize for literature in 1913. He wrote in Bengali but translated some of his poems, plays and stories into English. He was also a musician, and songwriter, and wrote the words for the national anthems of India and Bangladesh. Some of his poems, like 'Vocation', are his memories from childhood. He believed that a poem could be an offering to God.

Lord Tennyson
(1809-1892)

English Victorian poet. He became Poet Laureate (the highest honour for a British poet) in 1850. He was Queen Victoria's favourite poet. Some of his poems are about animals like 'The Eagle', 'The Owl' and 'The Kraken'. Others are based on myths and legends like 'The Lady of Shalott,' 'Ulysses' and 'Morte d'Arthur'. Some of his poems like 'Song', 'Flower in a Crannied Wall' and 'A Sea Shell' (p 28) are about the beauty and mystery of nature.

Chuang Tzu (3rd century BC)	Chinese teacher, philosopher and writer, who wrote stories and conversations to encourage people to think about life and nature. He did not not write his words as poetry, but many of his ideas are poetic. Two poetic stories for thinking are translated in this book as 'The Happiness of Fish' (p 45) and 'Who Dreams?' (p 80).
Walt Whitman (1819-1891)	American poet of the nineteenth century. He wrote in rhythmic free verse, and printed by hand his first book of twelve poems called *Leaves of Grass* (1855), adding poems to each new edition of the book until it was over 400 pages. His famous poem 'O Captain! My Captain!' is about the death of Abraham Lincoln. Other poems like 'Miracles' and 'A Child Went Forth' celebrate the wonders of everyday life.
William Wordsworth (1770-1850)	English poet, who lived in Dove Cottage in the Lake District. He was popular in Victorian times and was made Poet Laureate in 1843. He loved nature and wrote many poems about what he saw and loved. He wrote a long poem about his life called 'The Prelude'. His best-known poems include the sonnet 'Composed Upon Westminster Bridge', and 'Daffodils'.
Kit Wright (born 1944)	English poet for adults and children who writes about the unusual things in life, and about unusual people such as Dave Dirt and his dog, and Walter Wall the carpet salesman. His poetry books for children include *Hot Dog, Cat Among the Pigeons*, and *Rabbiting On*.

Acknowledgements

We are grateful for permission to use the following copyright material:

'Isn't My Name Magical?' by James Berry © 1994. Reprinted by permission of Peters Fraser & Dunlop Ltd on behalf of James Berry. 'Parrot' by Alan Brownjohn from *Brownjohn's Beasts* by Alan Brownjohn, published by Macmillan Children's Books. 'The Listeners' by Walter de la Mare, reprinted by permission of the Literary Trustees of Walter de la Mare, and the Society of Authors as their representative. 'It Was Long Ago' by Eleanor Farjeon, from *Silver, Sand and Snow*, published by Michael Joseph. 'The Road Not Taken' by Robert Frost, from *The Poetry of Robert Frost* edited by Edward Connery Latham, published by Henry Holt and Co., New York. 'A Boy's Head' by Miroslav Holub, from *Miroslav Holub: Selected Poems*, translated by Ian Milner & George Theiner, published by Penguin Books, copyright © Miroslav Holub 1967. Translation copyright © Penguin Books 1967. 'Friends' by Elizabeth Jennings, from *Collected Poems* by Elizabeth Jennings, published by Macmillan. 'A Poem Just for Me' by Roger McGough, from *Pie in the Sky* by Roger McGough, published by Penguin Books, reprinted by permission of the Peters Fraser & Dunlop Group Ltd. 'Back in the Playground Blues' by Adrian Mitchell, from *Greatest Hits* by Adrian Mitchell, published by Bloodaxe, reprinted by permission of Peters Fraser & Dunlop Ltd. 'Who Do You Think You Are?' by Carl Sandburg, excerpt from *The People, Yes* by Carl Sandburg, copyright 1936 by Harcourt Brace & Company and renewed 1964 by Carl Sandburg, reprinted by permission of the publisher. 'Vocation' by Rabindranath Tagore, from *The Complete Poems and Plays* by Rabindranath Tagore, published by Macmillan. 'The Magic Box' by Kit Wright, from *Cat Among the Pigeons: Poems by Kit Wright* (Viking Kestrel, 1987) copyright © Kit Wright, 1984, 1987.

The following poems in this book are the copyright of Robert Fisher: 'To Find a Poem', reprinted from *Another Fourth Poetry Book* ed. John Foster, published by Oxford University Press. 'Long After Humankind Has Gone' reprinted from *Minibeasts* ed. Robert Fisher, published by Faber & Faber. 'The Happiness of Fish' and 'Who Dreams?' by Chuang Tzu, translated by Robert Fisher.

Acknowledgements are also made to any copyright holder whom the editor has been unable to trace in spite of careful enquiry.